WORDS OF PRAISE FOR
WHAT'S YOUR EXCUSE?

After reading John Foppe's amazing story, you will never look at yourself in a mirror the same way again. To slightly paraphrase John, *What's Your Excuse?* is one great big hug to the heart!

—H. WAYNE HUIZENGA,
CHAIRMAN OF THE BOARD
OF AUTONATIONS, INC.

I met John Foppe at the National Leadership Forum in Searcy, Arkansas, June 2001. That meeting was profoundly moving for me. I have faced extreme hardship in my life, but I faced it as an able-bodied man. Seeing John cope with life's daily challenges with no arms made me feel sorry for him at first. However, I soon realized he does not feel sorry for himself. His book, *What's Your Excuse?*, is an expression of his positive, can-do approach to life. I very much admire a positive message. It is what I try to impress upon the people to whom I speak. Knowledge, understanding, faith, and a positive attitude are the tools of courageous, successful people. Reading John's book helped me understand what obstacles he encountered, daily challenges he overcame, and insights he gained along the way. These are all things we can learn from and incorporate into our daily lives. I recommend *What's Your Excuse?* to anyone who wants to take charge of life and be a survivor, not a victim.

—DITH PRAN,
SURVIVOR OF THE CAMBODIAN
HOLOCAUST, WHOSE STORY
INSPIRED THE 1984 ACADEMY
AWARD–WINNING FILM, *THE
KILLING FIELD*

Every one of us has survived some type of tragedy. John's story and practical insights help all of us to overcome the challenges in our lives. *What's Your Excuse?* is not just an inspirational book but a definitive "how to" guide for triumphing over our problems.

—DAVE PELZER,
NUMBER ONE
INTERNATIONAL BESTSELLING
AUTHOR OF *A CHILD CALLED
IT* AND *HELP YOURSELF*

John Foppe's book *What's Your Excuse?* is an inspiration just like he is for all those who have been touched by him.

—JIMMY JOHNSON,
FORMER NFL COACH, MIAMI
DOLPHINS AND DALLAS
COWBOYS

If you truly want to reach your goals. then you must read, *What's Your Excuse?*

—RUDY RUETTIGER,
INSPIRATION BEHIND THE
TRISTAR HIT MOVIE *RUDY*

WHAT'S YOUR
EXCUSE?

Making the Most of What You Have

John P. Foppe

OLIVER
NELSON
™

THOMAS NELSON PUBLISHERS®
Nashville

A Division of Thomas Nelson, Inc.
www.ThomasNelson.com

Published in Nashville, Tennessee, by Thomas Nelson, Inc.

Scripture quotations noted are from THE NEW KING JAMES VERSION. Copyright © 1979, 1980, 1982, Thomas Nelson, Inc., Publishers.

Library of Congress Cataloging-in-Publication Data

Foppe, John.
    What's your excuse? : making the most of what you have / by John Foppe.
        p. cm.
    ISBN 0-7852-6637-2 (hardcover)
    1. Success—Religious aspects—Christianity. 2. Foppe, John. I. Title.
  BV4598.3 .F66 2002
  248.4—dc21   2002000745

Printed in the United States of America

02 03 04 05 06 BVG 5 4 3 2

To Mom and Dad,

Carole and Ron Foppe,

thanks for your courage to do the

tough things and for your love

that eased the pain.

And to all my brothers:

Bill, Joe, Tom, Ron, Jim,

Patrick, and Paul,

thanks for the strength each

of you unselfishly gave me

in your own unique way.

CONTENTS

Foreword ix

Introduction: You Never Know xiii

1. Are Your Actions Speaking Louder
   Than Your Feelings? 1

2. What's Your Condition? 13

3. Are You Willing to Do the Last Thing
   You Want to Do? 25

4. Do You Genuinely Love Yourself
   Enough to Change? 35

5. So What's Your Style? 53

6. What's Your Position in the Game of Life? 65

7. What Are Your Chances at Making the
   Play-Offs? 85

8. How Big a Life Are You Willing to Pursue? . . . 99

9. Have You Laughed at Yourself Lately? 111

10. Are You Asking the Right Questions? 121

11. Are You Spiraling Downward or Upward? 137

12. Are You Aware That You Are
    Blessed to Be a Blessing? 153

CONTENTS

13. Are You Willing to Ask for Help? 169

14. Is There a New Possibility
    You Should Explore? 185

15. How Do You Choose to
    Walk Your Daily Journey? 193

Conclusion: The Answers Are Yours 201

Acknowledgments 203

About the Author 205

FOREWORD

What's Your Excuse? is a remarkable story about an amazing man raised by a delightful family, and the grace of God. Since I have known, loved, and worked with John Foppe for several years, I can tell you that you are in for a treat. John simply and beautifully shares his trials, tribulations, and glorious victories. I am always inspired when I see John in action. Most important for you, I believe you will learn that what God tells us in Romans 8:28, that "all things work together for good to those who love God, who are the called according to His purpose," is one of the great truths of all time.

As John states in his book as well as in his talks that are so well received all over the world, had he been born with the longest, strongest arms in existence he would still have been able to reach only so high or lift just so much. However, because God has blessed him (you read it right) with no arms, he has been forced to develop creative ideas that enable him to deal with more crises and challenges in a typical day than the average person encounters in a month. Yes, God does compensate us for our deficiencies.

You will weep, laugh, and express astonishment as John unfolds the details of his life in this book. I believe you will want to share this story with your friends, family, and associates, because it truly does prove that a life built on faith and centered on others can be significant.

Behind, underneath, alongside, and overall, as you read his words, a feeling of hope will permeate your own life, regardless of what your circumstances might have been or are today. You will take a new look at your own future, and be a better person and performer as a result. You will ponder in amazement how this young man can accomplish so much. Next you will realize that without the loving support and encouragement of not only his family, but the people God placed around him throughout his life as well, his future would have been different. The "tough love" John experienced from his parents, particularly from his mother, enabled him not only to survive but to thrive. You will come to believe that if he can, you can—that when you take "step one," God will put a new spirit in your heart and bring people into your life that will make it richer, better, and more exciting.

John is lovingly direct in his dealings with others, and faces his own challenges head-on as he encourages and inspires you to do the same. He is effective in doing this because along with the normal stresses of growing into maturity, John had far more challenges with the things most of us take for granted—like personal hygiene, eating, dressing, using the telephone, driving, functioning in public, learning to cook, etc. Through creative assault on every problem, John has been able to solve many of them.

John experienced phases of rebellion, stubbornness, anger, and self-pity as many kids do. However, he worked through all of them, much of it through necessity and some because he realized a better way would provide him with a better life. John recognized his limitations but spent his time developing his possibilities. You will discover that John learned what other kids did easily was often difficult for him and required more commitment, persistence, and determination, as well as more creativity on his part. He was forced to develop the qualities that would make him the outstanding contributor to society he is today.

I believe this book will substantially improve, perhaps even radically change, your life. That's why I believe *What's Your Excuse?* is "must" reading.

—Zig Ziglar

Introduction

YOU NEVER KNOW . . .

"WHEN YOU WAKE UP IN THE MORNING, YOU NEVER know where you will be by the time night falls."

I can't think of another statement that describes the totality of my life any better.

Those words certainly held true the day I was born. As Mom and Dad hurried to the hospital on a summer morning, they were hoping to deliver a healthy baby girl. Instead, they became parents of a sickly, disabled baby boy—a child born without arms. By the time evening fell, their lives were in chaos. When I was rushed into emergency surgery to repair an internal problem in my abdomen, they cried and worried that I might not survive. The odds were a million to one that I would die within days. Today, I am in my third decade of life.

A priest once refused to allow me to take a role in the worship services at my church. In contrast, I was summoned by Pope Paul VI during a visit to the Vatican and received a special papal blessing.

When I was ten years old, I relied on others to dress me. I led a life marked by dependency. On my twenty-sixth birthday, I put on a suit and necktie—by myself—and stood on a stage in Jakarta, Indonesia, to present a seminar.

As a child, I couldn't play football with my brothers. But I have been on telethons with the Dallas Cowboy Cheerleaders and have given a motivational address to the Miami Dolphins.

I once ached inside because I didn't have arms and hands to pick up a child who reached out to me in a developing nation. But in 1993, I was given a pair of hands . . . well, sort of. I was one of the youngest persons ever honored by the U.S. Junior Chamber of Commerce (Jaycees) as one of their "Ten Outstanding Young Americans" for the speeches I delivered to raise money and awareness on behalf of those living in Third-World poverty. The Jaycees' trophy commemorating this award is a sculpture of two *hands* reaching toward each other. Inscribed into the base of the award are the words, "The hope of mankind lies in the *hands* of youth in action."

My life reflects a tremendous balance of extremes. Your life may not have a pendulum that swings quite so broadly, but of this I am certain: you have lows and highs, problems and triumphs, limitations and strengths, liabilities and assets. We all do. I've come to appreciate an equal certainty: every time a door seems to be shut tightly, a window is waiting to be opened. Every time a problem seems to be unsolvable, an option, perhaps unusual or never before tried, is waiting to be discovered and pursued.

Every day, I face dozens of challenges. For the most part, they are practical ones about how to accomplish certain chores and tasks most people with arms, hands, and fingers would consider to be routine. Have *you* ever tried to break and fry eggs using your feet and toes? Have *you* ever driven a car using only your feet? Have *you* ever tried to dress yourself without using your hands? I have learned to cope with such challenges in innovative ways—and I hope, with an abiding courage to take risks, perseverance, and a well-developed sense of humor. Surely if I can find solutions to the practical problems I face, you can too!

I also face the same myriad of emotional, mental, and spiritual challenges that are common to all human beings. I face times of discouragement, times when I feel stressed out, times when I feel rejected, times when I wonder what the future will hold. If my master's degree in social work and my work as a counselor have revealed one thing to me, it's this: emotional challenges are far more difficult than physical challenges. Even so, solutions *are* possible.

I have a basic message: every problem has *some* type of positive resolution. Avoid the excuses. Find the resolution. Run with it. And enjoy both the challenge of the struggle and the reward of the accomplishment.

I hope my story will inspire you to recognize what I believe to be true for you, and what I know to be true for me: all things are within reach!

My odds of living were a million to one. What are your odds of living your life to the fullest?

One

"I HATE YOU!

"You are the worst mother in the world!

"I can't believe you are being so mean to me!

"You don't love me!"

Mom took it all in silence, a tear gently rolling down her cheek. She didn't respond, and she didn't move. She just sat on the edge of my bed as I spewed out a torrent of frustration, anger, and fear.

Sweat was running down my forehead and mingling with tears that were gushing from my eyes. With every belligerent word or phrase that a ten-year-old could utter, I demanded to know why my mother was being so cruel to me. "Why are you doing this to me?

"You know I can't get dressed by myself!

"You know I need your help. You know I need my brothers to help!

"You're a terrible mom!"

With each charge I bellowed at Mom, a new tear ran down her cheek. But she didn't yield.

Those few minutes were undoubtedly the worst minutes of my life to that point—not only for me, but for Mom. How had we reached this low point in our relationship?

The moment had been almost eleven years in the making. It was the end of a long crescendo that began even before I was born.

TROUBLE FROM THE VERY BEGINNING

Between the birth of my next-older brother and me, my mother had experienced a miscarriage. Her pregnancy with me was also difficult. She has written that she felt tired and restless much of the time, not happy and joyfully expectant as she had been with her three eldest boys. At the time of my birth, she was more than eager for the pregnancy to end. She had experienced ten months of pregnancy, two false labors, and two unnecessary trips to the hospital prior to my delivery. She suspected through it all that something was wrong— terribly wrong.

The look on Dad's face confirmed what she had suspected. His first words to her after she gave birth were, "Carole, I don't want to make the phone calls. I can't tell our parents."

At the time my mother was pregnant with me, there were no sonogram tests or other prenatal tests that might alert a parent to the possibility of physical abnormalities in an unborn baby. She had no medically based opportunity to prepare for my birth. My parents had been prepared, how- ever, in a way that I believe was a sovereign act of God on their behalf.

Four weeks before I was born, my parents went on a retreat weekend to Our Lady of the Snows, a national shrine near

Belleville, Illinois. The morning after their arrival, my father saw a priest he had not seen since childhood and invited him to join them for breakfast. Over steaming cups of coffee, my parents and Father Maronic shared the events of their lives, and the priest mentioned a support program he had initiated at the shrine for disabled people: Victorious Missionaries (VM). He asked my parents to help him start a VM chapter in their town of Breese, Illinois. They agreed, and two weeks later, they sponsored a meeting at their home.

That night, the conversation focused on a disabled child who had died a short while before. The child's father, an acquaintance of my father, had never mentioned the child. My parents were shocked to learn that night about a family in their small town who had a disabled child that they had not even known was born.

Before the meeting, my parents knew very little about disabled people and certainly had no personal experience with anyone who was disabled. In fact, my mother has said that all she knew about disabled people was that she wasn't supposed to stare at them. After the meeting that night, my mother promised herself that if the baby she was expecting wasn't normal, she would not hide the fact from her neighbors and friends. She would treat her exceptional child just as she treated her other children.

There in the hospital, as Mom actually faced the news that her child had been born with multiple disabilities, her first response to my father was one of courage, confidence, and determination. "Oh yes, you can make those calls," she said. "You're going to treat this baby just as you did the other boys. You go out and buy your cigars and shout the news from the housetop."

My dad squeezed her hand and went to make the calls he dreaded. My mother was left with his words ringing in her ears: "The baby doesn't have arms." Intuitively she had known something was wrong—but she didn't know the exact nature and extent of the difficulty even then. Alone in her private room, she reached into her purse and pulled out a mother's prayer manual she had brought with her to the hospital. She flipped through the pages and found a prayer for mothers of exceptional children and read it with new insight. Immediately she thought of Father Maronic and asked a nurse to call him. She wanted him by her side when she first held me. Twenty minutes later he walked into her hospital room and I was brought to my mother for the first time.

As the nurse gently placed me into her arms, Mom pulled back the blanket and saw the slick spots where arms should have been. All she could say was, "Thank God, he has legs!" She wrapped the blanket around me and handed me back to the nurse, and she and Father Maronic talked for a while about the miraculous "coincidence" that had brought them back into contact after so many years, and about the "coincidence" of my parents' budding involvement with the Victorious Missionaries project.

The tears came next. The confidence my mother felt in the first hours after my birth gave way to mourning the loss of a healthy child. She experienced deep, racking sobs as she came to grips with the reality that she was the mother of a child with serious health problems and physical anomalies. She felt herself sinking into dark despair and cried out to God, "Help me accept this!"

The three people who seemed to accept most readily the

fact of my physical limitations were perhaps the three most unlikely people: my brothers Bill, Joe, and Tom. Dad had taken a very direct approach in telling them that their baby brother was born without any arms. Billy, my oldest brother, asked why God would send the family a baby without arms. Dad answered, "Well, you see, son, God had this little boy without any arms, and He asked Himself, 'Now, who can I send this little fellow to and be sure he'll be cared for? Why . . . here is a family where he will have a home and three brothers to look after him.' So now we're going to bring him home and take care of him, but we may have to give up a lot of things in order to help him."

Billy responded, "Dad, he can have everything in my piggy bank . . . and he can have my allowance . . . and, Dad, we'll take good care of him." And from that very first day of my life, they did. Not the piggy bank contents and allowance, of course, but they did care for me in countless practical ways. They were exactly the big brothers I needed.

Did my parents ask what had caused my disability? Certainly. The only illness my mother had experienced in her pregnancy with me was a bad case of the Hong Kong flu when she was two months pregnant. The doctors thought that might be a possibility, although there was no way of knowing for sure. The *why* questions were ones my parents quickly realized they could not answer. And frankly the *what next* questions were the ones that needed their immediate attention.

The morning after I was born, the physicians informed my parents that my physical problems were more complicated than they originally thought. Surgery was required immediately to connect my upper and lower bowel. The surgery itself had a one-in-a-million survival rate since my abdominal cavity had already become septic. My parents had me baptized, and then I was rushed to Cardinal Glennon Hospital for Children in St. Louis, a little more than an hour's drive away.

Two weeks passed before my mother saw me again, because the doctor would not allow her to travel. My life was hanging by a thread.

My mother has told groups through the years how empty, vulnerable, and helpless she felt during those days of separation from me. She also felt totally unprepared for what she would see when she finally visited me at the hospital. She found my body twisted in the little hospital bassinet, with needles stuck into my legs, my back snarled by severe scoliosis, my eyes wandering.

A MOUNTAIN OF PROBLEMS REMAINED TO BE CLIMBED

My parents knew that the very fact that I had survived the surgery was miraculous, but in the wake of the miracle, a mountain of problems remained. Their newborn had no arms, severe irregularities of both hip sockets, a lazy eye, and a head that appeared lopsided.

They knew God must have a plan for my life, yet the enormity of the physical challenges that lay ahead clouded their recognition of what that plan might be.

My mother's first impulse at seeing her son in that hospital bassinet was to run away and hide. She felt intense conflict within—most of the time holding me and treating me with big doses of love and affection, but at times experiencing unexpected and unwanted feelings of repulsion. She felt pummeled by each new pronouncement from the doctors, perhaps the most devastating of which was their opinion that I would never walk.

Although I knew nothing of this at the time, of course, in retrospect I am very grateful for Aunt Marie. One day as Mom left yet another doctor's appointment with me, she sought sanctuary at Aunt Marie's house. My great-aunt always had an incredulous tone in her voice when she retold the story: "Carole stomped into the house, dumped that precious little baby on the dining table, and walked away. And I opened that blanket and Carole didn't have any clothes on him!"

Aunt Marie took care of me while my mother sulked in an adjacent room. She talked to me as she dressed me, "We're going to fix you all up. Let's put a little powder right here, and how about a little lotion right there. Here's your undershirt. Over the head we go. Now, let's slip on your handsome suit." Then she carried me in her arms to the rocking chair in her kitchen. She sat down and said to me in rhythm with the rocking motion of her chair, looking at me all the while but speaking to my mother, who was just out of sight but not out of hearing range, "We're going . . . to take him . . . just like . . . he is."

The total acceptance from Aunt Marie made it easier for my mother to accept me, just the way I was.

Just as my mother's courage had been displayed and then took a hit in the hospital, so my mother's acceptance of me took a hit a few weeks later. Neighbors across the street brought home a healthy baby girl. My mother and the neighbor had laughed and talked excitedly about the babies they were expecting, and my mother was determined to congratulate her neighbor when she knew that the woman and her baby had come home from the hospital.

As Mom crossed the street and reached up to knock on her neighbor's door, she realized her knuckles were white and her teeth were clenched. She felt a torrent of conflicting feelings as her neighbor, holding her newborn in her arms, answered the door. Through gritted teeth, my mother managed a stiff "Hello." Then she looked at the baby. With her beautiful black hair, the baby seemed perfect in every way. My mother saw in that little girl everything that she had hoped for me, and she crossed the street back to her own home feeling hatred and jealousy. She has said, "If feelings had a scent, I would have smelled vile in that moment."

In that moment my mother faced her feelings fully. She saw herself—with her clenched jaw, narrowed eyes, pinched brow, and grimaced face—and what she saw made her conclude that she was more deformed than her son! She felt ugly on the inside as well as the outside.

Again, Father Maronic came to her at Dad's request. She unloaded to him all the bitterness and grief she felt. Father Maronic put his arms around her and said, "Carole, these are just human feelings." He spoke to her at length about fear, and then he prayed with her and asked God to let her see His purpose for my life. My mother came to three tremendous and life-changing conclusions that guided her in the following years.

First, Mom came to a full recognition that feelings may come and go, but *actions* in the wake of feelings count.

Second, Mom came to believe that I was not incomplete. Rather, I was exactly as God had made me—a human being with full potential to be realized.

Third, Mom came to understand that her expectations for me were not nearly as important as the expectations I would come to hold about myself.

I cannot begin to tell you how crucial these three conclusions are for any person to draw regarding his (or her) lives and the lives of others around him.

ACTIONS MATTER FAR MORE THAN FEELINGS

What you do is vastly more important than how you feel. Most feelings we experience are temporary. They are usually based upon external circumstances and events, which are also temporary. Actions, however, have a lasting impact on self and on others. Actions—those things we actually say and do—become embedded in memory. Actions mold our reputations. Actions establish relationships and produce accomplishments.

Through the years my mother has given a number of speeches to various groups in Illinois and other states. People have asked me, "How do you feel, John, as you hear your mother describe the feelings she had about your birth and your disabilities?"

I respond to them very simply, "Her feelings were a normal part of being human. Her actions, however, are what made her a good mother."

I have never felt hurt by the feelings my mother might have had. If anything, I admire the fact that she didn't allow her feelings to dictate her actions. She *acted* toward me as a responsible, loving, caring, encouraging, and yes—even demanding—mother. She required courage and creativity from me, even as she responded to her role as a mother with courage and creativity.

Never allow feelings to limit what you choose to do. You can act in a positive way even if you don't feel positive. And the more you act positively, the greater the likelihood that positive feelings will follow.

Allow your will, your faith, and your long-standing dreams and goals to compel you forward. Don't be led by your emotional response of the moment or, as I like to say, "feelings du jour"—feelings of the day.

We chart our lives primarily by what we *do*.

Every one of us faces the challenge of discovering the unusual, potentially limiting conditions of our lives, and then learning how to stop those conditions from disabling our spirits.

Two

WHAT'S YOUR CONDITION?

As I TRAVEL ACROSS THE NATION AND IN OTHER countries, I have found that most people don't know how to respond to a person with physical deformities or physical limitations. As Americans, we still aren't even sure what to call a person who has deformities. We've gone from using the word *crippled* to *handicapped* to *disabled* to *physically challenged*, and, for the most part, we aren't comfortable with any of these terms. I personally choose not to be preoccupied with labels, but if I had to choose one word, I would choose *condition*.

The word *handicap* implies that something cannot be done. *Disabled* implies a defect or lack of ability. While that may be true in the strict sense of the word—physically—most people who have unusual physical conditions do not think of themselves as defective or deformed. What may be true in the physical sense is certainly not true in the psychological, mental, spiritual, or emotional arenas, which are the far more important realms of human existence.

The term *condition*, by definition, means "something indispensable to the appearance or occurrence of something else; a prerequisite, restriction, or modification." That about sums it up for me. I am restricted in some ways. My condition requires that I approach certain tasks in a different or modified way.

I have a physical condition. *I am not* a physical condition. The difference sounds minor but, in actuality, is major. My physical state—not me as a person—may warrant a label.

EVERY PERSON HAS ONE OR MORE CONDITIONS

The fact is, every person has one or more conditions. Some conditions are obvious to the observer—they are outward, physical, visible. Some outer physical conditions have profound impact on a person, although they may not be as obvious as having no arms. Consider the impact of these conditions upon daily functioning: poor hearing, limited eyesight, baldness, lack of coordination, color blindness, extreme allergies.

Other conditions are inner and private—grief, depression, loneliness, addictions. All of us have inner struggles from time to time, some more severe than others. Consider the impact of these conditions upon daily function: phobias of various types, worry, constant feelings of anger, obsessions, intense cravings.

Some conditions may be culturally imposed. Our culture is quick to label certain people as disadvantaged or in a less-than-ideal condition, such as "single parent," "minority race," "at-risk," "underprivileged," or "extreme."

Whether the condition is one we recognize as applying to ourselves or is a label imposed from the outside and a condition we do not choose to recognize, the challenge we all face is this: How can we stop the condition from disabling our spirit?

Figuring out how to approach the challenge of your particular condition is like plotting a journey on a map. You can't get to your intended destination unless you first know your location. Knowing your location is the same as acknowledging the existence of your present condition. Coming to terms with the condition or conditions you have and assessing their impact on your total life are the first steps toward understanding how to handle the conditions.

People frequently ask me, "John, how do you deal with having no arms?"

My answer is a mirror of their question: "I just deal with it."

I do what I have to do to compensate for my condition in order to get where I want to go and to get through that moment. I do what I must do to compensate for my physical condition in order to achieve the goals I want to achieve.

In that way, I am no different from you. If you are going to go where you want to go in life, experience what you want to experience, and achieve what you dream of achieving, you are going to have to deal with your condition in some way.

We face four choices every day:

1. Sleeping in
2. Caving in
3. Tuning in
4. Digging in

1. SLEEPING IN

"Sleeping in" is a passive choice. The person who opts to sleep in—not literally, but figuratively—may be so overwhelmed by his condition that he simply doesn't know what to do. It may also be the passive choice of a person who is in denial of his condition or who wants to ignore the difficulty of dealing with his condition.

I slept in one day in the fifth grade. At that time, I was still dependent on others to help me use the rest room. My teacher was having a bad day and was very irritable. I knew that I would have to ask another student to leave the classroom to go with me to the rest room, and the combination of those two challenges—asking my teacher for permission and asking another student to go with me—was just too overwhelming. I did nothing. And finally I couldn't hold it any longer, and I wet my pants. Doing nothing turned out to be a lot more devastating than ignoring the warning signals my body was sending me!

The person who sleeps in gives up before trying. He does *nothing*. There's a woman in my hometown who takes this approach. For the past ten years she has refused to have her cataracts removed. Consequently she is practically blind, and she expects her six children to look after her. Each adult child takes a turn "mom sitting." To complicate matters, she injured her back a year ago, and she continues to experience pain from that injury. Although the family's commitment to their mother is admirable, she has slept in on taking responsibility for her health. She refuses to see her doctor. Anytime someone asks her, "How are you doing?" she replies, "Everything is fine." The fact is, things *aren't* fine. She's in denial.

The sleeping-in pattern may be a literal pattern. The person may drift through days by sleeping, watching TV, idly talking on the phone, playing video games, or doing any other activity that at the end of the day has resulted in nothing accomplished, nothing truly gained materially, financially, socially, mentally, or spiritually.

Sleeping in, in its most extreme form, means failing to take any personal risks or failing to accept any responsibility for your own life. It's a position in which you expect others to make decisions for you, take care of you, and continue to provide a world in which you might sleep peacefully and awaken to have all your needs provided. It's a position of allowing others to shoulder the burden of your support, both financially and emotionally.

Sleeping in is an attempt to escape a condition.

Sleeping in is an option we all have. I heartily recommend, however, that you don't choose that option!

Are you willing to wake up and embrace your life—all of it? Are you willing to face the conditions in your life and seek ways of dealing with them?

2. CAVING IN

The person who "caves in" recognizes his condition and is overwhelmed by its enormity. He does not try to deny the condition. Rather, he is so fearful of the condition that he is paralyzed by it.

Are you aware of how lions hunt? In any pride of lions, there is usually one dominant male lion and several lionesses and their cubs. When it comes time to hunt, the role of the male lion is primarily to roar. He circles an isolated or weak animal, periodically letting loose a giant roar that causes the prey to become disoriented and paralyzed with fear. The paralysis born of fear keeps the prey from moving with the herd. Then the lionesses can move in quickly for the kill.

The person who caves in has allowed the roar of his condition to paralyze him into doing nothing positively.

The trouble with doing nothing positively is that it soon leads to doing something negatively in response to the condition—generally speaking, to doing something to dull the roar of the condition.

Negative responses tend to take one of two courses. The first course involves blaming others: "My sister didn't give me the message," "My pager must not be working properly," or "My job has put too many demands on my life to deal with this condition—I just don't have any time left for myself."

The second course involves doing something to try to blot out the reality of the condition. That course may involve the use of alcohol or drugs. It may be a flight away from a job or away from a community or city in an attempt to outrun the condition.

A story about my great-great-grandpa Heinrich Foppe has taken on almost legendary qualities in our family. It seems Heinrich was a farmer who had a vineyard. He made home-made wine from the grapes his vineyard produced, and he stored his wine in barrels in a cellar under his house. When Heinrich became overwhelmed by the enormity of any situation, he retreated into his "cave" or cellar and drank himself into oblivion. One day his wife found him passed out in the cellar from drinking too much. She became so disgusted that she drained all the wine barrels. When Heinrich came to his senses, he asked her what had happened to all his wine. She replied, "You must have emptied all the barrels in your drinking spree." He had no recourse except to take her word for it!

The person who caves in is scared of the challenge of taking responsibility for his condition and for his life. He is afraid he will fail. Not wanting to be called a failure by others, he seeks to put the blame for failure on someone else or to run from the situation.

The person who caves in never wins the game because he's too scared to play it.

Are you willing to move beyond fear and explore the options that are available to you for dealing with the conditions of your life?

3. TUNING IN

The person who chooses to "tune in" honestly assesses his condition and his ability to contend with the hurdles it represents, and then begins to tune in to solutions, alternative methods, and innovative answers.

Tuning in requires a person to say to himself: *Here's the condition, here are the multiple options I have for overriding this condition or compensating for it, and here is my chosen way of responding.* Tuning in involves identifying the condition, surveying options, and making choices.

Tuning in nearly always means tuning out some things. You can't listen to two radio stations at once and fully understand either. Neither can you pursue multiple goals at once with equal energy and equal success. I cannot drive a car and wave hello to someone at the same time. I can, however, do each task one at a time. Tuning in requires focus. It requires sequencing tasks and prioritizing objectives.

A few years ago I gave a speech in Puerto Rico for an insurance company, and my brother Jim accompanied me. We spent a couple of extra days vacationing on the island, and one of those days, we toured the Arecibo Observatory. This observatory has the world's largest single-unit radio telescope. The antenna structures can be moved in any direction to track a celestial object. This powerful instrument has been used to produce detailed radar maps of the surface of Venus and to plot information about the rotation of that planet. The telescope is tuned in.

In like manner, we need to tune in to our own selves from time to time to discover how better to deal with the conditions of our lives. As far as I am concerned, tuning in is the first step toward dealing with any condition positively.

For me, the time I spend painting helps me tune in to what is deep inside me. When I was growing up, I was very jealous of my older brother Tom, who is a very talented artist. My sixth-grade teacher, Rita Page, challenged me to explore my own artistic ability. She told me I needed to stop comparing myself to Tom and to stop trying to paint in the same style he painted. She encouraged me to explore my creative talents, and I am very grateful to her for her encouragement. Painting is therapy for me. It allows me a medium for processing my thoughts and feelings. I have a quiet place reserved outside my bedroom where I keep my painting supplies open at all times, and I usually have a piece of artwork in progress. Painting is my time for tuning in to process my thoughts and feelings, my dreams and goals.

Tuning in opens the channels for creativity to flow in many different ways. Newton tuned in when he saw an apple fall, and the result was a better understanding of gravity. Galileo watched the great swing of a lamp and tuned in to the idea of using a pendulum to measure time. Watt was in his kitchen when he noticed steam lifting the top of his teakettle, and he tuned in to the idea of a steam engine.

Are you willing to focus on the next-best move for your life? Are you willing to tune in to your deepest needs, ideas, and creative urges to come up with the options that are right for you?

4. DIGGING IN

"Digging in" is running with the option you have chosen for dealing with your condition in any particular circumstance or environment. Not all options work in all settings. But chances are, at least one option will work.

That's the approach I took when it came to wearing ties. I didn't wear ties as a young teenager, but when my speaking career began to bud and I was asked to speak in formal settings, I knew the time had come for me to figure out how to put on a suit and tie.

Obviously I couldn't tie the tie with my toes while it was around my neck. I knew there had to be another way, so I dug in and explored my options with Mom and Dad. We tried tying the tie in advance so all I had to do was slip it over my neck and pull the slipknot tight. That sounded good in theory, but in reality, it didn't work very well. The knots tended to lose shape and look sloppy, and occasionally a knot would come completely undone.

Through trial and error, we finally hit on a solution. Dad tied one of his old ties around my neck at the appropriate length. Then Mom cut off the section of the tie that was around the back of my neck, leaving only a small tab of material on either side of the knot. Next, Mom sewed Velcro onto those tabs and underneath the collar of my shirt. The tie sticks on underneath the shirt collar, and no one can tell that it doesn't go all the way around my neck.

This method allowed me to buy any tie I found appealing. I tend to like expensive ties—those from Brooks Brothers are my favorites—so I had to be willing to cut up several ties as I experimented. But by digging in I found a solution that allowed me to travel and dress myself even for formal events without any assistance.

Digging in is a psychological choice that is made repeatedly, sometimes many times in a day: "I *will* move forward in my life in a *positive way*. I *will* deal with my condition in order to do what I want to do, experience what I want to experience, and achieve what I want to achieve."

One of my aunts died recently from complications related to cancer. Although her death was tragic, she was a vivid example to me of someone who dug in and fought the good fight. My aunt was diagnosed with cancer fifteen years ago, and she chose to fight the disease with all her ability. She was willing to consider every option and do whatever was required.

She had a breast removed. When the cancer continued to spread, she went through all of the conventional chemotherapies. All along, the doctors didn't give her a very positive prognosis, but she refused to accept their opinion that she was dying. When chemotherapy had run its course, she allowed physicians to try experimental medicines and techniques. When those avenues were exhausted, she ordered herbs and explored alternative medicines. She dug in and lived longer than anyone expected. She was dancing at Oktoberfest three months before her death!

In my opinion, it is highly unlikely that a person will truly dig in unless he has a set of goals that he considers worth pursuing.

Are you willing to pursue with diligence and enthusiasm the best forward-motion move for your life?

THE BEGINNING OF GROWTH

The person who chooses to sleep in does not grow. Neither does the person who caves in. The only person who grows is the person who tunes in to the conditions of his life, seeks out the best possible solutions for overcoming them, and then digs into pursuing the solutions.

There have been countless times in my life that I could have slept in or caved in. I have chosen, rather, to tune in and dig in. What's your choice?

The first thing you need to do is often the last thing you want to do.

Three

EVEN IF I HAD BEEN BORN WITH ARMS, MY BIRTH would have created a problem for my parents: I was their fourth son, and the house in which we were living was small. It was apparent to them that they would need a bigger house for their growing family. Within a year and a half of my birth, they began to search for a new house.

Mom was immediately attracted to a stately old Queen Anne Victorian home in an older neighborhood of our town. She liked the five spacious bedrooms, the large yard, the inviting wraparound porch, the beautiful craftsmanship of the interior, and the gigantic and stately European beech tree that stood like a sentinel guarding the front door.

The house had been built by A. C. Koch and his wife, Ada, in the early 1900s. Koch had made good money as the owner of the Breese Mill and Grain Company, and the Queen Anne home was their dream house. A. C. died in 1956 and his wife in 1972. After Ada's death, the Koch children put the house up for sale, and my parents expressed an immediate interest.

The more they studied the house, the more they could

envision themselves raising their family in it. They negotiated a price with the Koch family and agreed to purchase the home. Before any papers were signed, however, Mom and Dad decided to walk through the house with my mother's parents, Elmer and Henrietta Stukenberg. Dad and Grandpa examined the foundation and windows from the outside. Mom and Grandma explored the interior. They rolled open the heavy pocket doors that separated the living room from the dining room. They marveled at the carved built-in cabinets in the butler's pantry. They climbed the thirty-two steps up the stately staircase from the main floor to the bedrooms on the second and third floors. They explored all the nooks and crannies throughout the house. Mom was excited with the idea of living in the house, but Grandma was more reserved.

After the two women finally completed their tour of the house, they descended the stairs and paused to rest on the seat built into the bottom of the stairway in the reception hall. Mom took note of Grandma's quiet mood and said, "You're not saying much. What's wrong?"

Grandma hesitated for a moment but then stated her concern, "Carole, I know you're excited about this place. It's truly beautiful. But, honey, you don't even know if Johnny will ever walk. How would he contend with all these steps?"

Psychologists today would probably call what Grandma did a reality check. From my mother's perspective, it was a dousing of cold water on her glowing flames of enthusiasm. Her heart sank as she knew her mother was speaking with a voice of reason. The house that seemed a wonderful distraction from the complications and tensions of her life held within its walls the likelihood of causing even more complications and tensions for me, and therefore, for her.

Although I was learning to use my toes to pick up and hold things, I would not take my first step until I was twenty-two months old. My parents had spent the better part of a year and a half taking me to doctors and visiting me in hospitals while I was probed, prodded, and examined. The doctors had voiced serious doubt that I would ever walk because of the deformities in my hip joints. Various physicians had wrestled with the option of placing pins in my hips to strengthen the growth of the bones. Other physicians recommended that I be fitted with artificial limbs as soon as possible so that I could adjust to the use of prosthetic devices from an early age. My parents made countless treks to the Shriners Hospital in St. Louis. And in the midst of it all, the conclusion was obvious. A house with bedrooms on the second and third floors might be a dream, but it was not the right house for my parents and a nearly two-year-old son who had no arms and could not walk.

Mom and Dad backed out of their agreement to buy the house—disappointed to be sure, but equally certain they had made the right move.

Did my parents give up the idea of living in a larger home? No. They needed to give up their first idea, however, before they could move on to their better idea. They needed to do what they didn't want to do.

The answer for my parents was a twenty-acre apple orchard in timberland ten miles outside our small hometown. There they built a home near a serene pond that rests between two rolling hills. We moved into the house about three years later. Trails through the woods led to Shoal Creek, which still winds behind the house.

My parents designed a modern home equipped with sliding glass doors, a feature they believed would allow me to open and close the doors more freely with my shoulders. At the time the construction was completed, I was five years old and about three and a half feet tall. As a result, all of the house's light switches were lowered to three feet from the standard four feet so I could turn them on and off with my shoulders. Mom chose lever door handles so I could open the interior doors easily with my chin or shoulders. My parents meticulously sought to eliminate or modify any feature of the home that they thought might create an obstacle for me later.

Meanwhile, I learned to walk. And very soon after, I began to learn the lesson my parents had learned:

> Sometimes the first thing we *need* to do
> is the last thing we *want* to do.

THE DIFFERENCES BEGAN TO EMERGE

My mother had a phrase she'd use when she became exasperated with my brothers and me for our nagging, whining, or fighting. She'd say to us, "You kids go outside and let the stink blow off of you!"

When my brothers and I heard that expression, we knew Mom meant business. We'd better hurry outside!

By that time in our family life, outside was the country around our new home built in the orchard. My parents also had two more sons—Ron, born three years after me, and Jim, a baby at the time of our move. With six boys underfoot, I think the only way Mom could maintain her sanity at times was to chase us older kids outdoors.

Not that Bill, Joe, Tom, or I minded. We still had much to

explore in the wilderness surrounding our home. Sometimes my brothers hopped on their bicycles and sped off down the trails into the woods. Other times they jumped into the family canoe and floated across the pond in search of snakes and frogs. Sometimes they climbed the branches of the apple trees and hurled unripened fruit at one another. These outdoor adventures seemed to bind my brothers together, but at the same time, they tended to set me apart from them. I couldn't climb a tree, ride a bike, or paddle a canoe.

About the same time that the outdoor play was making me feel separate from my brothers, I began school. The stares and questions from my classmates dislodged the comfort shield that the hugs and affirmation from my family had created. I felt increasingly awkward and left out. It was hard to fight back the tears when I had to sit on the sidelines of the playground, wishing I could tackle the swing sets and monkey bars.

I began to feel that everyone knew something I didn't know . . . that my peers were ahead of me somehow, and that I didn't fit in with the kids at school as I had always seemed to fit into my family. While the other kids played, I tagged along behind the parent who was the playground monitor for the day.

Rainy days were my favorites. On those days, we played games on the classroom floor during recess, and I could participate more fully at that level. There were never enough rainy days, however, to drive away the feelings of fear and pity that were starting to take root in me.

More and more, I found myself thinking, *I don't want to be different . . . I don't want to bother the other kids . . . I'm afraid to try that. What if I fail?* More and more I focused on the things I could not do with my feet, and the list was pretty long:

- I couldn't dress myself or undo the buttons on my coat.
- I couldn't use the bathroom facilities by myself.
- I couldn't ride a bicycle, bat a baseball, or handle a pair of scissors.
- I couldn't catch a football.
- I couldn't tie my own shoes.

The more I focused on my limitations, the more frustrated I became. The frustration, in turn, gave way to resentment and self-pity. Before long, I was a stubborn and pensive child with a prevailing mind-set: "I can't."

My kindergarten teacher, Mrs. Niebruegge, noticed those "I can't" words coming from me more frequently. She sensed I was withdrawing from classroom life, and she attempted to reach out to me by reading the story of *The Little Engine That Could* to the class. I think she secretly hoped that I would take the moral of the story to heart and become more willing to try new activities.

A short while after she read the story to the class, she asked me to do something for her. I don't remember the exact nature of the task, but I do remember my reply. I looked her in the eye and said, "I think I can . . . I think I can . . . I think I can . . . but I don't want to."

Mrs. Niebruegge and my parents laughed at my willful declaration. Nevertheless, behind the words was a statement of brute honesty that I don't think any of us recognized at the time. I didn't *want* to try.

Most people I know would like to say, "I don't want to" to their family members or their supervisors at work, to the government or other public institutions. "I don't want to drive a car full of kids to school this morning!" "I don't want to stay late tonight, nor do I want to come in early tomorrow morning!" "I don't want to pay my taxes. And I sure don't want to drive at this ridiculous speed limit!"

Life is filled with things we don't want to do. Not wanting to do something, however, is not always a good reason for failing to do it. I was about to learn that lesson in full force.

FRUSTRATION TURNS TO ANGER

Coupled with my frustration at not being able to do certain things—and not wanting to try to do other things—was a growing anger. Ultimately that anger was aimed at God more than at any particular human being.

I remember one incident in which my older brothers were building a tree house. I could only stand below and watch as they climbed up into the branches and worked together to make a place that seemed distinctly their own. I hated God for making me without arms and cried myself to sleep that night asking, "Why me?"

Now, I never denied the existence of God. I was quite sure God existed. I just cursed Him for the way He made me and for the way He stacked the odds against me. I flat out didn't like what God had done to me and had no notion whatsoever that He might be on my side in any way, shape, or form.

That night was not the only night I railed at God or asked Him, "Why me?" What began as an act of feeling sorry for myself became a pattern of self-pity. I desperately wanted Him to help me—and very specifically I wanted Him to give me arms. Yet I figured He didn't care about me; and therefore, I couldn't count on Him to do *anything* for me. I was struggling with the enormity of the possibility that I would have to live without arms for the rest of my life.

The more I felt sorry for myself, the more I focused on the things I couldn't do, which in turn made me feel even more sorry for myself. The spiral was down, down, down until I ended up on what I call a pity pot. When a person ends up on a pity pot, self-esteem virtually evaporates.

When you become totally consumed with what you aren't, can't do, and don't have, it's nearly impossible to feel worthy or valuable. If you are struggling with self-esteem issues today, I encourage you to take a long look in the mirror and ask yourself, *Do I dwell more on the negatives of my life or the positives?* If you're honest, you're probably going to have to admit that you think a lot more about what you aren't, can't do, and don't have instead of the positive attributes of who you are, the many things you can do, and all of the resources, material goods, and skills you possess.

THE MOMENT ULTIMATELY COMES

The moment ultimately comes when frustration and anger must vent. At that point, a person faces two options. He can unleash like a volcano and destroy a great deal, including relationships he deeply values and perhaps even his own life. Or he can turn the negative energy of his frustration and anger into the positive energy required by change.

It's a matter of love. Do you love yourself? Do you love others? Do you love God? If so, you are going to take the steps to change. If you don't, God help anyone who has to live with you.

What's the last thing you want to do?

Do you love yourself enough to make changes?

The price you are willing to pay to fulfill your dreams is proportional to the value you place on yourself.

Four

Do You Genuinely Love Yourself Enough to Change?

As I progressed through the early years of grade school, I felt increasingly beaten. No matter how hard I tried to fit in, I tended to come away from situation after situation feeling limited and different. I had little desire to challenge myself, and I had frequent arguments with my parents about wearing my artificial arms.

I received a new pair of artificial limbs as I started grade school. The old hooks I had been given and taught to manipulate as a toddler were replaced by rubber "hands" that were dyed to match my flesh tone. Fingerprints were actually embossed into the fingers of the hands, and blood vessels were painted on the wrists and back of the hands.

Although the prosthesis looked quite natural, especially from a distance, the device was heavy and cumbersome. The limbs weighed about ten pounds—a significant weight for a sixty-pound child—and wearing them made me sweat profusely.

In function, the artificial hands were only slightly improved over the hooks. The fingers worked as a single unit and pressed together with the thumb like a claw for picking up items. The wrist could rotate 360 degrees, and the elbow was jointed. All of these functions were manipulated by a sequence of twitches I had to learn to make with my shoulders and upper chest muscles.

Even though the artificial arms made me look more like other kids, the apparatus was a constant annoying reminder to me that I was different. I refused to wear them routinely.

I remained dependent on my family to help me get dressed and to use the bathroom. I had absolutely no motivation to learn to do those things for myself.

In an effort to help me become more independent, Mom and Dad offered ideas for adapting my clothing. I didn't want any part of that. Adapted clothing was just one more sign to me of difference that I was unwilling to accept.

Then Mom and Dad introduced me to Dr. Harold Wilke, a minister who was born without arms and who traveled all over the world. My parents were hoping that he would inspire

Photo by Jim Kennett

John signing his autograph while wearing tabi socks.

me about my future, and that I could learn to apply some of the techniques that he used to live independently.

Dr. Wilke visited our home and explained many of the practical ways he made it through an average day. One of the main things he shared with us was his method for being able to go to the bathroom without any assistance. Because he wore highly elastic suspenders on his pants and did not wear underwear, he was able to pull down his pants with the toes of one foot while standing on the other leg. Since he didn't have hands to tuck his shirttails into his pants, the tails of his shirts were cut off so they were square at the bottom. Dr. Wilke also wore Japanese tabi socks. Like mittens for feet, tabis separate the big toe from the rest of the toes. The design allows the wearer to pick up and manipulate items with his toes.

I wanted nothing to do with those ideas! I was certain that wearing tabis, and especially wearing suspenders, would only establish another distinction between me and the other kids at school. I was fearful of having to explain to anyone that I needed the suspenders in order to be able to go to the bathroom without assistance. In addition to those reasons, I felt sure my brothers would occasionally snap those suspenders just to aggravate me. Most of all, I was angry that I had to deal with such challenges. The fact that I needed assistance in going to the bathroom and tucking in my shirt made me embarrassed, angry, and frustrated—all at the same time.

By my fifth-grade year, I had developed a rather openly defiant attitude toward virtually everybody. I became so obsessed with my physical challenges that I began to fail science and math. My negative attitude manifested itself in obstinate, rude remarks to my teacher at school and my parents at home.

My parents were in the throes of parenting two more sons. My brothers Patrick and Paul—twins—were born in 1978. When I tell audiences that I am one of eight sons, I can always sense a combination of awe and compassion for my parents!

I personally have deep respect and admiration for my parents in their decision to have more children after my birth. Mom and Dad must have feared another pregnancy, since they didn't know with certainty what caused my condition. They had no guarantees that other children would be born free of disabilities. Nevertheless, they did not allow fear to control their lives. As an adult, I regard their decision to have more children as a significant statement of hope and a powerful statement about the value of life. Each of my younger brothers' births was a proclamation to the world that life goes on despite uncertainties.

As a child, of course, I was too obsessed with my condition to care about my brothers. If I had any conscious thought about my younger brothers' births, the thought was probably one of relief. My parents were so busy with my twin brothers that they didn't have much time to pressure me to do things for myself. I could continue to count on my other brothers to help me in numerous ways, with very little bickering.

Then things took an abrupt turn.

THE WONDERFUL ALLURE
OF CAMP ONDESSONK

One afternoon at school the principal called all of the fifth, sixth, seventh, and eighth graders to the gymnasium to listen to a speaker tell us what it would be like to spend a week at Camp Ondessonk, a summer youth camp in the Shawnee

National Forest of southern Illinois. I vividly remember him telling us about sleeping in log cabins, going horseback riding, taking an overnight hike, learning to build a campfire, and playing a game called Pioneers and Indians. The adventure sounded incredibly wonderful to me as a fifth-grade boy who didn't like his current life. What a marvelous escape from my reality!

I had heard about the camp from my older brothers who had attended in previous years. I was sure my time had come for this grand experience.

The remainder of that school day seemed interminable. I couldn't wait to get home with the slip of paper that had been handed out at the school assembly. I ran into the house and immediately spilled out the news about the camp and the school assembly to Mom. I recounted every detail I could recall, and then, brimming over with enthusiasm and anticipation, I asked Mom if I could go to the camp.

For a moment, she stood still, and a blank expression came over her face. I sensed immediately that something was wrong. Finally in an almost hollow voice she said, "We will talk about this after dinner." I had no clue what she was thinking, but somehow I knew not to push the issue.

As my brothers washed the dishes after dinner, Mom and Dad slipped out onto the back deck to drink their coffee. My brothers never gave their departure from the kitchen a second thought, but I had a strong hunch they were going outside to talk about my going to camp. I let my curiosity get the best of me, and I peeked out the door and saw them sitting together on the porch swing, sipping coffee, and staring out into the night. I walked out onto the deck and asked if they were ready to sign my camp permission slip.

With a deep breath and a casual glance at Dad for support, Mom said, "Johnny, you can't go to camp."

My heart started pounding, and tears flooded my eyes. I raised my foot to my face to wipe my tears. Gasping for breath, I asked, "Why?"

"You're not able to take care of yourself. You can't even go to the bathroom on your own," she said with disappointment. "I don't know the answer, John. We've tried to give you ideas. We've showed you how Dr. Wilke uses suspenders to help himself, but you won't listen and you refuse to try anything."

Still gasping and pouting, I managed to assert, "None of those things work for me!"

Mom responded, "You don't know that. You haven't tried to make them work. If you aren't going to use his method, you're going to have to figure out your own way of getting dressed by yourself and going to the bathroom by yourself. We've all tried to help you. I'm tired of fighting with you. It's up to you."

Dad added, "If you get an idea, John, about how to change something around here so you can better help yourself, tell us. We'll adjust the house or your clothing to do whatever it takes for you to become more independent. But there's going to be no more of our doing things for you."

I couldn't believe what I was hearing. Somewhere between anger and disbelief, questions started pounding in my head. *What are my parents trying to do to me? What does Mom want of me? Why is this happening to me? What's Dad talking about?*

Although I was deeply upset at what I heard, I could not fully grasp my parents' resolve in that moment.

I went to bed early and cried myself to sleep—the primary reason for the tears was that I had been denied the great adventure of going to camp, but some of the tears were ones of apprehension about what my future might hold.

While I was asleep, Mom called all my brothers together. I don't know how things worked in the home where you grew up, but in my home, Mom made the practical rules for us kids. If Mom wanted to change the rules, well, Mom changed the rules! That night, the rules were changed.

Mom lovingly explained to her other sons how my bad attitude was getting me into trouble at school and was preventing me from helping myself. She told my brothers they had no choice but to stop helping me so I could learn to do things for myself. She stated her case plainly: "If John has to run around naked until he learns to dress himself, then we'll have to let him go naked."

She acknowledged to my brothers that denying me help would be difficult. She was equally certain that if the entire family pulled together to help me in this way, I would benefit. Then she added the inevitable threat of punishment: "If either your Dad or I catch one of you boys helping John, you will be disciplined."

I had no idea all this was being discussed while I slept. To say the least, I faced a rude awakening the next morning.

A SWIFT AX AT THE ROOT
OF MY SELF-PITY

My younger brother, Ron, and I shared a bedroom, and as I was getting ready for school the next day, I asked him to pull up my pants. He started to approach me with a helping hand as he had always done in the past. From the time I could remember, my brothers had helped me get dressed without much fuss or argument. That time, however, Ron froze. A look of fear came across his face as if he had just seen a horrible monster standing behind me. I stood there waiting for him to move, my pants around my ankles.

"Well, are you going to help me?" I asked him with confusion and aggravation at his hesitation.

Ron ducked his head to break eye contact with me. "I can't," he said.

"What do you mean you *can't?*" I demanded.

He replied, "Mom said we aren't allowed to anymore."

"Aren't allowed to *what* anymore?" Even as I asked the question, I knew the answer.

"We're not allowed to help you anymore," Ron said.

His words rang in my ears like a death sentence. Indeed, in a way, the old Johnny was about to die. As I look back on that morning, I know that I had dreaded hearing those words all my life. I intuitively knew that Ron's defiance was not mere orneriness toward a brother. Mom was behind the tactic, and I experienced an avalanche of emotions. I felt hurt and betrayed. I couldn't believe my family was being so mean to me. I felt abandoned and rejected.

It was one thing for Mom to deny me permission to go to Camp Ondessonk. It was entirely another matter for her to turn my brothers against me.

The feeling that somehow I was being separated from my brothers was perhaps the ultimate hurt of all. I desperately wanted to be one of the guys. I had wanted that from my first memories of being a brother. So what if they had to help me get dressed and go to the bathroom? They didn't seem to mind. I didn't see anything wrong with having their help. From my perspective, Mom was creating even more division among us, calling attention even more markedly to the ways in which I was different from other members of the family.

Immediately I called out to Mom to see if she had really told my brothers they couldn't help me. She came into my bedroom and sat down on the side of the bed in the corner of the room. I tore into her verbally.

The memories of that confrontation with my mother are crystal clear. As I recall that time, I realize my tongue-lashing hurt Mom more than I could ever have known. I am forever grateful, however, that she had the courage to endure the release of all my pain without giving an inch.

"I hate you!

"You are the worst mother in the world!

"I can't believe you are being so mean to me!

"You don't love me!

"Why are you doing this to me?

"You know I can't get dressed by myself!

"You know I need your help. You know I need my brothers to help!

"You're a terrible mom!"

I yelled. I cried. I used every obscenity and said every hurtful thing I knew to say at ten years old.

When I finished my tirade, Mom silently got up and walked from the room. And I was left alone with my problem. How was I going to get dressed without having any arms, hands, or fingers to assist in the process?

I couldn't just stand there naked all day. I had no choice but to *try*.

Putting my feet in the legs of my pants, I lay down with my back on the floor. Then I raised my feet into the air and allowed gravity to do its work. Sure enough, the pants fell down to my hips. I swiftly lunged to my feet in a reverse squat and assumed a bull-legged stance. With my knees pushed out from each other, I was able to keep the pants up around my hips. But then what to do?

I looked around the bedroom for something that would snag the waist of my pants when I rubbed my hips against it. I waddled over to the dresser and tried to hook the belt loop of the pants on a stubby knob secured to one of the dresser drawers. I stood on my tiptoes and pushed my hips against the dresser. The chest shifted, and the lamp and knickknacks on it wobbled. I raised myself up on my toes again and again in an attempt to get my belt loop on the knob, but without any success. *If only I were an inch taller, then I could snag my pants on that knob.*

By now I was flustered and sweat started pouring down my face again. The salty sweat burned in my eyes. I knew that if I brought my legs together and raised one foot to wipe away the perspiration with my toes, the pants would drop to the floor. Instinctively I squeezed my eyes together to keep out the sweat. As I stood there half dressed, with my eyes closed, panic set in.

Panic was quickly followed by anger and frustration. *I can't do this. I know this won't work,* I thought repeatedly. I wanted to scream for help but I was repulsed by the thought of letting my brothers see me in this pitiful position. Finally I could stand the pain of the salt in my eyes no longer. I raised my left foot to my eyes to wipe away the perspiration, and my pants dropped around my ankles. I was back to square one.

I sank to the floor. The carpet scratched my naked back as I again raised my feet into the air. The pants fell to my hips a second time. I rose to my feet again. I searched the room for something else to rub my hips and pants against. The knob on the double-hung closet door caught my eye. I waddled over to the nook, shut the door with my foot, and leaned against it. My body weight stressed the door and I heard a cracking sound, but I was getting close. The knob was just the right height. I gently rubbed the belt loop against the knob. I didn't want to break the door out of its frame. To snag the pants on the knob, however, I needed to push harder against the door.

Once again, sweat began to pour, and my heart started to pound. The moisture ran down my back and waist, but I managed to hook the pants on the doorknob. *Finally*, I thought with relief. I squatted down so the pants would pull up around my hips. They moved some, but my clammy skin prevented them from sliding completely over my hips up to my waist. I cautiously tugged some more, but suddenly the belt loop slipped off the knob and my pants fell to the floor. I had failed again.

I dropped to the floor in exhaustion.

In that moment, I was left without clothes on my body, and I was stripped of my defenses. Everything seemed to have conspired against me—not only Mom, but the height of the knob, my body sweat, the weak closet door, the tight pants around my hips. I felt overwhelmed and utterly defeated and drained.

I had no more angry thoughts to feel, no more defiant words to say. I had felt all the anger I could feel and had said all the defiant words I knew to say. I just sat on the floor gasping for breath as tears poured down my face. My mouth was dry, my nose was running, and I felt as if the room were closing in on me. I was emotionally tapped out as I curled up in a fetal position in a pool of sweat and tears. Time seemed to stand still for me in that moment—it was the loneliest moment I have ever felt.

There's something to be said for complete emptiness. As uncomfortable as it may be, total emptiness frees us in some ways. It allows greater clarity of thought and new insights.

As I remained alone, naked, at the end of myself, I had a knowing deep inside me that I was tired of being angry. For so long, I had been my own worst enemy. I hadn't just been at odds with my teacher or my parents. I had been at war with myself—and with God. The anger I had expressed toward my friends and family was just a reflection of the real anger I felt against my Creator.

But where had my anger brought me? To the floor, naked, alone, and stripped of all energy, all defenses, all assistance.

In that moment of total defeat, I looked up and saw my reflection in the mirror. My tearstained face was red and had a beaten look. Then I noticed the short stubs of flesh hanging from my shoulders. And in that moment, I accepted that the miracle I had so desperately wanted wasn't going to happen—I was *not* going to grow new arms. I also came to the point at which I realized that my anger at God had brought me no relief, only further pain.

In the stillness of that epiphany moment, I felt God's presence all around me. In my heart, I heard Him softly say, *If you let Me, John, I will help you.*

I said, "Yes."

Something powerful, and I believe divine, happened to me in that moment. I no longer faced my problem alone. I made the first move away from being stubborn and toward being strong.

There is a fine line between being stubborn and strong. Both are fueled by a strong will, but to be stubborn is to be negative and to be strong is to be positive. When we are stubborn, we fight ourselves. We tear down our self-esteem and allow negativity to take control of us from the inside out. In contrast, when we are strong, we fight the condition that threatens to limit us. We acknowledge our feelings, look for options, take responsibility, and forge ahead. One of the most important lessons I have learned in my life began in that moment of silence before God: I stopped fighting myself and, with God's help, started fighting the problem I faced.

Over the next few days, I became willing to make changes. Mom altered my shirts so they were like the ones Dr. Wilke wore. I conceded to wearing suspenders and Japanese tabis. Dad installed a little knob at just the right height so that I could use my belt loop to pull my pants up around my waist. I began to gain independence.

And I finally did get to go to camp.

TOUGH LOVE ISN'T ONLY SOMETHING WE SHOW TO OTHERS

A lot has been written and said about tough love. I not only comprehend the concept of tough love . . . I know the *experience* of tough love. I not only know what it's like to be the recipient of tough love; I have a visage for tough love: Mom.

Mom had the ability to look past the pain she might be causing me in the immediate moment of my life and focus on the freedom that she knew I could enjoy if I were physically independent. Mom had an intuitive understanding that with every "yes" there is a "no," and conversely, with every "no" there is a "yes." Saying "yes" to a new pursuit requires that to some degree a "no" is said to old pursuits. Saying "no" to something can give freedom to say "yes" to something else. In saying "no more help for Johnny," Mom was providing a "yes" for many opportunities that lay ahead for me, all of which required greater self-reliance.

It took courage to do what my mother did that day. It took *real* love for her to take the risk of further exacerbating my problems in an effort to lead me to the point at which I might take responsibility for resolving my problems.

Years later, Mom explained to me that she knew if she didn't exhibit tough love to me in that moment, she would have been selfish. Like all parents, she wanted her son to love her, like her, and have fun with her. She didn't want to cause me pain, nor did she want me to think ill of her. But tough love required Mom to put aside her desires and to do what she knew was best for *me*. *Sometimes the first thing we need to do is the last thing we want to do*. Once again in my mother's life, the thing she needed to do was the last thing she wanted to do.

Mom gained courage in that moment by recalling the words of Jesus: "Take up [your] cross, and follow Me" (Matt. 16:24). For Mom, forcing me to come to grips with my condition was a type of "cross" for her. It was a type of sacrifice and trust. She had to sacrifice some of her peace of mind and peace in her home, trust God that her tactic would work, and move out solely on faith that what she was doing would end positively for *me*.

I have come to recognize that giving tough love hurts the giver far more than the receiver. Many people have heard their parents say to them at times of discipline, "This is going to hurt me more than it will hurt you." As children, we never believed our parents! As adults, we know they were right. No one wants to be the target of someone else's scorn, contempt, hatred, rejection, or pain, but at times, it's simply the right thing to do. And even more than right, it's the healing, helpful, *best* thing to do.

Yes, Mom was a source of tough love to me, and I give her a tremendous credit for the freedom and self-reliance I have today. I have learned through the years, however, that it isn't enough to be the recipient of tough love from another person. The real challenge—and one that we all face—is to love ourselves enough to perform tough love on ourselves.

The ultimate tough love occurs when we choose to be tough on ourselves in order to reverse a negative trend in our lives or get rid of a habit that is holding us back from meaningful achievements.

This concept of tough love lies between the wishes and fantasies that most people have about their lives and genuine success and accomplishment. Most people I know have vivid and often fabulous dreams about what they would like to do in their lives. Such dreams can function like a spark plug— they can get us started toward greater self-fulfillment. But without tough love, we do not have the fuel of discipline to turn dreams into concrete plans, plans into schedules, and schedules into the reality of day-by-day achievement. It is only when we choose to challenge ourselves, require things of ourselves, put demands upon ourselves, that we press forward. Only as we continue to choose to press forward do we overcome the obstacles that may lie in our path.

Without tough love we don't develop the habits necessary to accomplish the things that are worth doing. It takes consistent discipline to have excellent health, a well-trained mind, a deeper spiritual life, lasting friendships, or a career marked by distinction and reward. It takes discipline to continue in the face of crises, troubles, or delays.

It is tough love to say to self, "I am worth the energy and effort that this challenge requires."

It is tough love to say to self, "Get up and get going."

It is tough love to say to self, "I may have to do without some sleep, some luxuries, and some fun to accomplish this task, but I *will* do it because in the end, it is what I want to have accomplished in my life!"

Tough love isn't about power or control or manipulation. It is about doing what is ultimately *best*. It is requiring an extra effort or a new approach to overcome an existing negative, which may be a self-destructive habit, a pessimistic mind-set, or a demeaning label. Tough love is about positive change and positive growth. It is about developing one's potential for greatness rather than allowing that potential to dissipate or lie dormant.

TOUGH LOVE POINTS TOWARD A POSITIVE FUTURE

Ultimately tough love does not estrange. Rather, it engages a person in positive behaviors and positive thoughts. In a family situation, parents may be motivated to withhold certain privileges from a child to help that child face his unruly or delinquent behavior and make changes. A parent who takes this approach needs to hold out rewards to the child for good behavior, and point the child toward positive behaviors, positive attitudes, and positive goals.

It isn't tough love to push the child out the door, lock it behind him, and throw away the key. That's not tough love—that's abuse. Tough love is saying to a child, "Here's what I want you to do. Here is the reward you will experience for doing it. I'm here to help you, but I won't make these changes for you. I believe *you* can make these changes and become the person *you* genuinely want to be, and I'm here to help you make the changes." Tough love is best administered with a big dose of tender loving care.

The same principles hold true when we administer tough love to ourselves. It isn't tough love to look in the mirror and say, "You're worthless. You need to change because you are no good the way you are." Rather, it's tough love to look at one's total life with objectivity and *love* and say, "I'm going to become the person my Creator truly made me to be."

Set goals for yourself that are achievable and incremental. Set rewards for yourself—frequent rewards that are linked to incremental goals—and then actually reward yourself as you reach your goals. See the change process that you have embarked upon as an opportunity for genuine growth and development *as a person*. See the discipline and extra effort you are requiring of yourself as being directly linked to your deeper joy in life and noteworthy achievements in the areas that matter most to you.

Not everybody desires to have stacks of money, own fancy things, or be at the top of a corporate ladder. But everybody I have ever met desires something more than what he presently has. That something may be better health, deeper friendships, a more joy-filled inner peace, a better marriage or family life, a more satisfying sense of accomplishment, an enlarged ability to help others, a finer reputation in the community. Whatever that "something more" is in your life, you are going to have to love yourself with a tougher love to gain it.

Do you really love yourself that much?

Every person has a unique style that is worthy of full expression.

Five

SO WHAT'S YOUR STYLE?

WHEN I WAS ONLY ABOUT SIX MONTHS OLD, MY parents sat me on the dining room table and left me to my own devices. I wasn't all that mobile so they had little fear of my falling off the table. What they hadn't counted on was a toothpick lying within my reach.

My parents were engaged in conversation when one of them suddenly noticed that I had picked up the toothpick with the toes of my left foot. I not only picked it up, but I turned it over a couple of times with my toes, and then I lifted the toothpick to my face so I could get a better look at it.

In that one brief moment, my parents realized that I was capable of doing a great many "normal" things—just in a special or different way.

In lots of ways, I was an average kid. I learned to swim and eventually enjoyed doing flips off the community swimming pool's high dive. I liked to draw and paint. I wasn't that fond of math, but I was a better-than-average student.

Not everything in my life was doom and gloom. Some things were "perks." I got my picture in the paper more than my brothers—and I enjoyed the notoriety that came with being the one chosen to switch on the community Christmas tree lights or the one selected to help draw attention to fund-raising telethons.

Even though at the time I was born my brother had offered the money from his piggy bank to help me, that offer never really materialized. Still, I benefited in another way. My aunts and uncles were so eager to watch me use my nimble toes to put dimes and quarters and pennies into my own piggy bank that they'd empty their pockets every time they came to visit. My brothers got a little jealous because I seemed to get all of the loose change floating about the family. Deep down, however, they understood that my aunts and uncles were trying to compensate me a little for my condition and they didn't say much, at least until they wanted a loan.

I couldn't play a violin or a clarinet . . . but I was able to use my artificial arms to play trombone in the school band for a while.

I couldn't manipulate a push lawn mower very well . . . but as a child, I did great steering a lawn tractor with my feet.

I couldn't ride a bicycle . . . but I could drive an old golf cart that had been refurbished and was given to me by a generous, very mechanically minded great-uncle.

I couldn't carry a lunch tray from the cafeteria line to a table . . . but I could clutch a hot dog and bun, and pop open a soda can with my toes.

I could jump on a trampoline and ice-skate . . . help Mom by measuring the ingredients necessary for homemade spaghetti sauce . . . and brush my own teeth. For everything I couldn't do, there were dozens of things I *could* do.

My friend since kindergarten, Neil, once told a reporter,

"Everything John does was kind of weird the first time we saw him do it. Then we got used to it. After a while, we didn't even notice he had no arms. It was just John."

"LOOK MOM, NO HANDS!"

At the age of sixteen, I did what many teenagers do—I went to the local Department of Motor Vehicles and got a driver's license.

Yes, I drive a car. I can drive any vehicle as long as it has automatic transmission and power steering. I drive by using my left foot to steer and my right foot to operate the gas and brake pedals.

One of the high moments of my teen years was being able

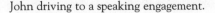
Photo by Jim Kennett

John driving to a speaking engagement.

to joke to my family and friends as I sped down the driveway, "Look, Mom, no hands!" I had waited several years to shout that line from an open car window!

The car I drove as a teenager was a brown '84 Chevy. I called it my "Vette." It wasn't a Corvette, of course. It was a Chevette. But it was mine to drive.

My friends always asked me to drive them to the mall. There was a very practical reason other than the fact that they liked having me around. I had handicapped license plates!

Actually, a career in motivational speaking seemed a real possibility the first time I was pulled over for speeding. The officer who approached my car said, "Buddy, I've been waiting for you all day." I responded, "I got here as fast as I could!"

I then asked the officer to get my license out of my wallet. It was the first time he noticed I didn't have any arms. He told me to slow down and sent me on my way.

I STILL HAVE MY "SPECIAL WAY"

Even today, I have my own personalized "special way" of doing the chores that other people consider to be routine. I don't really think about how others accomplish routine tasks. I simply go about my life *doing* them.

I probably follow the same routine that you follow in the mornings:

I make my bed. I just do it by standing on the mattress and using my toes to pull and straighten the sheets.

I dress myself. I just have clothes that are adjusted in minor ways and a small knob mounted in my closet—the only "adaptive" item in my entire house.

I shave myself. I just do it by sitting on the floor in front of a low mirror that extends all the way to the baseboard, using my feet to hold my electric razor.

I comb my hair. I just use my toes to grip the brush as I raise my left foot to my head.

I cook. I keep all my dishes in the lower cabinets and the frequently used food items on the lower shelves of my refrigerator. I use a high barstool when working at kitchen chores involving the sink, countertop, or stove. The added height of the stool allows me to sit at the same level as the counter in order to manipulate various types of kitchen equipment. Your Mom probably told you to wash your hands before preparing or eating food. In my case, I scrub my feet.

I may not be able to wear a watch on my wrist . . . but I certainly can wear one on my ankle.

I may not be able to adjust a speaker's microphone on a platform . . . but during breaks in my talk, I can take sips of water from a glass mug on a small stand to my side.

I may not be able to give you a physical hug . . . but I can hug you with my heart.

FINDING YOUR OWN WAY OF COPING

Once we face our shortcomings squarely, we are free to embark on the things we need to change. Once we stop fighting our own selves, we can start fighting the condition we have. Once we stop running from our problems, we can start overcoming our problems.

As we find our own ways of coping and adjusting and compensating, we experience the real joys of learning. And with the joys of learning often come related joys of laughing and loving.

Every one of us has to find our unique style for "doing things."

I live in an old home that was designed and built by others. However, I have painted and furnished my home differently from the previous owners.

That's a good analogy for what most of us face in our lives. We are born with certain "givens." Some of those are the givens of our physical bodies. Some of those are the givens of family, environment, and cultural heritage.

Each of us has to "paint and furnish" our givens with our own unique personalities and desires and ideas. We are ultimately the ones responsible for the "design" of our own interiors.

Shakespeare said it well, "To thine own self be true" (*Hamlet*, Act 1, Scene 3, Line 78). For me, that refers not only to my destiny and mission in life, but to my own style— my own special way of doing things.

THE DECISION NOT TO USE ARTIFICIAL LIMBS

One of the major milestones in my life came the day I decided I would no longer wear prosthetic arms. Period. As I have indicated, I always found the prostheses cumbersome and awkward to use. I tended to use them sporadically, and in many cases, I used them to aid the comfort level of *others* far more than I used them to aid myself. In the end, I realized that there was nothing I could do with the artificial arms and hands that I couldn't do with my chin, upper body, teeth, and toes—generally, more efficiently and quickly and with fewer negative "side effects."

I once was working with an occupational therapist on

picking up and manipulating various objects. One of the objects was a fairly large plastic pitcher filled with water, which I was able to pick up and hold. I turned to the therapist to express my pride in picking up this object and in the process, not only dropped the pitcher, but dropped it in a way that the water went flying out of it and soaked her blouse. The therapist benevolently and generously responded, "Well, I guess we haven't practiced that handoff enough." I appreciated her kindness but the fact remained: in most situations I had to practice far more with prosthetic devices to master simple maneuvers than I did with my own feet, toes, teeth, and chin.

In many ways, the prosthetic devices were cosmetic. They gave me a greater appearance of being physically normal, when in fact, I wasn't physically normal and, ultimately, I knew it and others knew it.

That isn't to say I'm not grateful to those who tried to help me by paying for and outfitting me with artificial arms. The St. Louis Variety Club purchased a couple of pairs of battery-operated artificial arms for me at a cost of more than ten thousand dollars. The arms were custom made, using parts and technology from all over the world. The arms strapped around my rib cage and shoulders and were activated by buttons I could touch with my chin. The hands opened and closed, and the arms raised and lowered. They were a "technological wonder." I just found them to be more of a hindrance than a help in the long run of my life.

I had to discover what worked for *me*. I'm still making those discoveries. I suspect you are too.

Through the years—mostly through trial and error—I learned:

No arms does not mean no ability.

No arms does not mean no compassion for others.

No arms does not mean no intelligence.

No arms does not mean no friends.

No arms does not mean no opportunities.

No arms does not mean no potential.

Having arms—even ones that looked fairly realistic—was not the foremost factor related to my success. Ability, compassion, intelligence, friends, opportunities, and potential were the real foundation stones on which to build my life.

You may not have something you think is vital to *your* success. Let me reassure you—you have plenty on which to build success! Take a look inside, not outside.

EVERY PERSON HAS A UNIQUE STYLE TO DISCOVER AND EXPRESS

There are any number of self-discovery books that proclaim a basic truth: every person is born with a unique potential. Every person is born with a set of gifts—natural talents, potentialities, desires, dreams, innate abilities, personality factors. Every person has "strengths" that deserve to be developed, nurtured, and used.

At the same time, *every* person is born with a set of flaws and conditions. Every person has something that must be overcome, endured, or counteracted. Every person has "weaknesses" that challenge a person to be creative in coming up with compensating or mediating actions.

I add this as the John Foppe corollary: every person has a unique style waiting to be discovered and expressed. Every person has built into himself or herself a particular "way of doing things" that needs to be valued and developed.

It's as we discover our own special "style" for doing things— everything from the way we express ourselves verbally to the way we choose to dress or fix our hair—that we

- come up with our own unique solutions to our unique problems.

- learn how to live noble, decent, productive lives that are personally fulfilling and exciting.

- find ways that work for us in dealing with the problems that we cannot solve but must live with.

The story is told about two men who were traveling a mountain road. As they rounded a bend, they discovered that a landslide had covered the road. To the left was the steep mountainside, to the right was a sheer drop into a valley far below. Before them lay a pile of rocks and shrubbery that had been pulled from its roots.

"Well, I guess we'll just have to go back," one man said.

The other replied, "No, we must go forward. This is the only road over the mountain."

"But how?" the first man said as he stared at the landslide in their path.

His companion replied, "We have one of four choices. Climb carefully over those rocks. Climb the mountain to our left until we are beyond the landslide and then work our way back down to the road. Drop over the edge of this cliff as we carefully seek out toeholds and handholds. Then we'll need to inch our way along the face of the cliff until we get beyond the landslide. Or we can tunnel through the rocks."

The first man nodded. "I'd rather pray for dynamite or wings."

There are times when we each would like to have dynamite to blow up the obstacles in our pathways. The trouble with dynamite is that it's difficult to control and we have just as much chance of doing damage to ourselves as we do to the problem. The dynamite approach to problem solving usually creates more problems than it solves!

We'd all like to have wings at times so we might fly away from obstacles that fall into our lives paths. The problem with wings is that we can't grow them and we wouldn't know how to use them even if we could. Those who live in a fantasy land of denial rarely accomplish much in life.

The wisdom and reality of life are that if we are to reach our potential, we are going to have to climb over, tunnel through, or find a way around our problems. We are going to have to face squarely both our strengths and weaknesses, and then find a way to use our strengths to overcome our weaknesses. Those things are choices we make individually—there are no pat formulas that work for every person.

The fact that I have no arms makes me no less of a *person*. I *have* a condition—it doesn't have me.

Being armless doesn't limit my *style*. I have talents, abilities, traits, and strengths that have nothing to do with having arms—an artistic eye, a creative mind, an ability to organize ideas and express them, a willingness to try, the courage to persevere, a good sense of humor, an ability to make and sustain friendships, faith with which to establish a relationship with my Creator, a family to love, and a desire to become more than I presently am.

The challenge facing me is the same challenge facing you as you seek to fulfill your potential: to identify your strengths and discover your own style.

Know what it is that your Creator built into you—identify your talents and innate abilities, isolate the dreams and desires that you have had from childhood, focus on those things that you have a special aptitude for doing.

Take a look at the resources that are available to you. Those resources come in the forms of family members, friends, mentors, encouragers and faith-builders, and teachers, as well as resources that may take the forms of instructional programs, travel experiences, and conversations with those who might be considered older and wiser.

Find ways of marshaling your strengths and your resources into solutions that work for *you* and that allow you to climb over, burrow through, or bypass your weaknesses.

We each face the challenge of leading with our strengths . . . and doing so with a unique, highly personalized style.

There is a big difference
between an excuse and an
explanation. An excuse is offered
to seek a way out of a challenge.
An explanation is offered to
seek a way into a solution.
The distinction between an
excuse and an explanation
lies in your motives.

Six

WHAT'S YOUR POSITION IN THE GAME OF LIFE?

I CLEARLY RECALL THE DAY I CAME HOME FROM bowling with my friends. As I shared the experience with my parents, they quickly picked up on the fact that I had been relegated to the position of scorekeeper while the other kids bowled. They insisted that the next time I went, I try to bowl.

After the next bowling excursion, I proudly informed Mom and Dad that the kids had put the ball on the floor and I pushed it with my foot. And I scored a strike! I naturally got a lot of gutter balls, too, but so did my friends.

Much of what we do in life is determined by one simple choice we make: to play, or not to play. In countless situations, in countless ways, we face the choice of whether to participate or sit on the sidelines.

Before we are willing to make the choice to participate, we usually have to deal with the excuses we generate for ourselves about why we can't, shouldn't, or won't participate.

We generally offer excuses to keep others from thinking we are selfish, lazy, or ill-willed. We can also use them to gain sympathy. As a boy, I became quite good at using excuses in that way. When people saw that I had difficulty grabbing or holding something, they tended to jump in and handle the challenge for me, or they excused me from further trying. Looking back, I can recall a number of times when I chose to excuse myself from a challenge or took an easier way out.

Excuse-making came easy for me on Saturday mornings. My brothers helped Dad with the outside chores, such as mowing the grass and cutting firewood. I stayed inside and read a book. There were certain chores I *could* have done, but I hid behind my excuses instead.

Later, my parents caught on that I was capable of doing more than I said I could do, and I did get my share of chore assignments. While my older brothers cut the grass and my younger brothers pulled a few weeds, I was responsible for watering the flowers.

EXCUSE OR EXPLANATION?

There's a big difference between an excuse and an explanation. An excuse is offered to seek a way out of a task or responsibility. An explanation is offered to seek a way into a solution.

The primary distinction between an excuse and an explanation begins at the level of motivation. What do you want? Do you want to run from the condition, difficulty, or challenge? Or do you want to run toward a solution, a goal, or a reward?

Those who opt for excuses and who, as a result, run from their problems soon discover that their problems follow them. As the saying goes, "Wherever you go, there you are!"

Intense emotions such as fear, resentment, bitterness, and anger do not dissipate in a cloud of excuses. Rather, these emotions become entrenched deep within you the more you offer excuses or the more you seek to run from your problems. You may be able to suppress these feelings for a while, but eventually they will erupt in some way, and the eruption often has negative consequences for you and for others around you.

However, if you engage in explanations aimed at finding a solution, you tend to find solutions. When "I can't do it, so leave me alone" is replaced by "I can't do that, but I'd still like to participate, and there are other things I can do," progress can be made.

Excuses focus on limitations that can cause failures. Explanations focus on a balanced assessment of limitations *and* assets, and the shift toward assets can bring success and rewards.

I had a burning desire to be one of the guys or part of the team. I wanted to participate. I knew there were some things I couldn't do, but there were also some things I could do. When I shifted from excuses to explanations, more opportunities to participate opened up.

For example, I might not have been able to play games that involved extensive use of the hands, but I could play games that involved running and feet. Yes, I became a soccer player. I wasn't the fastest runner on the team, and I played only a few years, but I did play. I belonged to a team, and I helped score goals.

Nearly all group games require scorekeepers, timekeepers, umpires, or referees. I could blow a whistle, watch a clock, and keep track of statistics. I could take part, I just couldn't play every part.

Frankly that's the story for most people.

I've met people who love music but are tone-deaf and can't

keep a beat. Does that mean they can't be involved in producing music, attending concerts, managing concerts, or running a music store? No!

I've met people who love a particular sport, but they aren't the least bit coordinated or talented as a player of that sport. Does that mean they can't work as an announcer, write for a newspaper, own a sporting goods store, or coach a team of youngsters in that sport? No!

Find your niche. Find the role you *can* play.

Generally speaking, we all play four roles from time to time:

1. Escapist

2. Aggravator

3. Spectator

4. Participator

In each role, we have an opportunity to offer excuses or come up with explanations that include assets as well as limitations. Each role can be approached from a negative or a positive angle.

1. THE ESCAPIST "SITS THIS ONE OUT"

The escapist completely checks out of a situation. The escapist chooses not to face his destiny, and passively allows life to pass him by.

The negative escapist tends to withdraw from the day-to-day world and blends in with the countless lonely people who live on the margins of society. I feel the greatest compassion for the negative escapist because he usually has experienced tremendous pain or disappointment at some point in his life. He may have tried to overcome his condition without much success and therefore feels defeated. He may feel there is no place else to turn. He may be suffering from feelings of hopelessness, inadequacy, and low self-worth.

The positive escapist may simply need a break, a time for relaxation or renewal, a time for reflection or further education, a time for personal growth or involvement in urgent and demanding matters (such as health crises or family difficulties). The positive escapist recognizes that he cannot be all things to all people at all times and that there are times for rest and rejuvenation in order for times of work to be more productive and effective.

At still other times, the positive escapist knows that it is better to leave a situation than to remain in it. He knows that growth lies elsewhere, and he sees no positive contribution that he can make by remaining in a bad or degenerating environment. He may have the good sense to walk away from a bad joke, a string of failures, or an error in judgment.

I had an opportunity a few years ago to assume the role of escapist, and I trust I did so in a positive way. I had been living in Dallas for a couple of years, although in retrospect, I was hardly ever in town. I spent much of my time on the road giving speeches and conducting seminars, and my time in Dallas tended to be devoted to catch-up or planning work at the office with very little chance to become involved in a church or engage in other activities I enjoy. Given my travel schedule, I had few occasions to forge deep friendships.

For several months, I asked myself more and more frequently, *Why do I live here and not back in my hometown?*

Certainly there was a downside to moving back to my hometown. I couldn't help questioning, *Would this be perceived as a failure by me, as well as by others, that I could not live independently? Would Illinois be a good place for me to meet new people and make new business-related contacts? Would it be a place of growth or stagnation for me?* Breese, Illinois, is a small town, and having grown up there, I knew very well the Cheers phenomenon: everybody knew my name. There are advantages and disadvantages when everybody knows your name and thinks he knows *you*.

Nevertheless, I had very good friends and a loving family in Breese. I knew my way around town, and there's something to be said for calling in a food order to Wally's, the local hamburger joint, and saying only, "This is John Foppe. I'll have my usual." I knew I would be within an hour's drive of a major airport for the travel my work requires, and I would be within a half hour's drive of excellent shopping, restaurants, and entertainment.

The questions remained, however: Was I escaping my present reality of feeling disconnected because I couldn't manage life in a big city, or was I escaping my present condition of loneliness in order to embrace a more fulfilling life—one marked by a home of my own instead of an apartment, and involvement in community activities where I truly felt I could make a difference on a local level?

In the end, I decided that I really wouldn't be losing anything by returning to Breese. I made the move, and as it turned out, I was right. I have maintained a good working relationship with my former employer—providing services as an independent contractor rather than an employee—and I have been able to maintain contact with people I came to value in Dallas. Was I escaping Dallas? Yes. Was it a positive escape move? I certainly believe so.

Here is the key question to ask yourself when playing the role of escapist: *Am I escaping the reality of my life or escaping a current situation or circumstance so I might better embrace the future I desire?*

2. THE AGGRAVATOR KEEPS THE POT BOILING

The aggravator stirs the pot and, more than that, tends to turn up the heat to keep the pot boiling.

When this role is played negatively, the aggravator becomes a person who criticizes others and incites conflict. He dwells on limitations and tends to major on the minors. He often is cynical of life in general and tends to have a litany of reasons for why all change is bad change.

The aggravator is a small thinker who tends to see the world through the singular lens of his own likes and dislikes. He is rarely a pleasant person to be around. People tend to avoid the aggravator, which in turn only makes the aggravator more aggravated and aggravating!

Perhaps the two most damaging words an aggravator utters are these: "You can't . . ." At times, he may switch to saying "You won't . . . ," "You shouldn't . . . ," or "You'll never . . ." I pity the child who grows up in a family where one or both parents are aggravators, constantly telling the child, "You won't ever amount to anything," "You shouldn't try," "You'll never achieve your goal," or "You can't make it out there on your own."

Although there have been times in my life when I have told myself honestly and candidly, *I can't do that,* I have never liked other people telling me I can't. As a child, when I heard, "You can't . . . ," I tended to launch a defiant offensive to prove that particular aggravator wrong. I especially chafed under aggravators who said, "You can't . . ." with a condescending or pity-coated attitude or tone to their voices.

As an adult, I have only a slightly different reaction to the aggravators who say, "You can't . . ." Although their statements are often phrased in more polite language, they ask, "Do you really think you're up to that?" or, "I don't know if I would do that if I were you." I still chafe at the attitudes of condescension and pity, but I also am more realistic in asking myself, *What am I trying to prove here? Is doing this really worth the time, effort, and energy? Is this person looking out for my best interests?* The answers to such questions are important, not only for me but for everybody.

Certainly we should weigh criticisms and heed cautions. We should digest words of wise advice and we should establish priorities in life. Not everything that can be done needs to be done or should be done.

Sadly, however, most aggravators are *not* looking out for the best interests of those they criticize or demean. They are attempting to put down someone else or deny someone else an opportunity in order to elevate themselves or make their lives easier.

One of my first experiences with an aggravator occurred while I was still in grade school. I attended a Catholic school, and one day near the end of the school year, one of our parish priests announced that he was recruiting new altar boys. I was excited at this prospect, and I believed that being an altar boy was something I could do. I saw it as an opportunity to be one of the guys.

The following afternoon, those of us interested in becoming altar boys were dismissed from class for an orientation meeting at the church. The priest showed us the specific duties that had to be performed at each part of the service. I listened intently, but subconsciously I was worried that he would make an issue of my condition. He didn't say anything to me, however, and at the end of the session, he took down each of our names and sent us back to school.

As I was shuffling out of the pew to head back to school, I heard my name being called. The priest and I were the only two remaining in the church. He asked, "John, do you think you're going to be able to do this?"

With an edge of panic in my voice, I answered, "I'd like to give it a try. I promise to use my artificial arms."

He broke eye contact with me, stared at the floor in hesitation, took a deep breath, and said, "OK."

I walked back to school with a lump in my gut. A lot of unanswered questions raced through my mind: *How was I going to do it? Who would be willing to be my partner? Would the pastor work with me?* Despite my self-doubt, I did not want to be turned away from the activity. I was determined to give it my best effort and find a way to be successful.

The school year ended, and nothing more was said about my serving as an altar boy. Every Sunday that summer, I couldn't wait to check the servers' schedule at church for my name. Weeks went by. I saw my classmates' names appear on the list, but not mine. I tried to wait patiently. I continued to hope, *Maybe next week!* Sunday after Sunday, I searched the schedule for my name, but it never appeared.

Finally I faced the fact that my name wasn't going to appear. I learned that the priest had never put my name on the altar-boy list. I was crushed by his rejection. Even more than hurt, I felt aggravated. He hadn't given me a chance! He had dismissed me without letting me try. He had put me down in order to avoid any embarrassment a failure on my part might have caused him.

I learned in the experience that aggravators don't necessarily need to say or do anything. Sometimes their lack of speaking or lack of doing can express volumes.

Is there a positive role for aggravators? You bet. One of my favorite quotes comes from Edmund Burke: "The only thing necessary for the triumph of evil is for good men to do nothing." We need aggravators to confront injustices, to right errors, and to combat evil. People such as Gandhi and Martin Luther King Jr. were positive aggravators.

Aggravators protest social ills until they are resolved, voice objections until unfair practices are changed, and refuse to be denied what is fair and equitable. Aggravators stand up for the deserving underdog.

I have benefited from my brothers taking the role of aggravator at times. If a person in a public setting is unkind to me, I rarely say a word. That's usually because I can't get a word in edgewise. My brothers or my friends immediately speak up for me.

That happened at the time of my junior prom. My date and I went to a very nice restaurant for dinner. I wore my artificial arms that night, but as always, I felt hampered and uncomfortable. It was a real struggle to try to eat with them. Finally my date—a very nice girl I had known all through our school days—said, "John, why don't you just eat the way you usually do? It'll be a lot easier."

I agreed. So did the others at the table. There, in my tuxedo, sitting at a nice restaurant with a white tablecloth, fine china, crystal, and silver, I slipped my foot out of my shoe and proceeded to use the toes on my left foot to hold my fork and raise my water glass.

The waiter rushed over to the table and with a haughty tone to his voice said, "Young man, this is a reputable establishment."

Before he could utter another word, the negative aggravator found himself confronted by a table full of positive aggravators. The waiter was told directly and forcibly that I had no arms and that they didn't mind my eating in a way that was natural for me and also natural for them to be around.

The trouble with being an aggravator is that we often do not see ourselves taking this role. Those who engage in negative aggravation tend to justify their behavior by saying, "I'm just being truthful," or "I'm trying to maintain high standards," or "I'm trying to save everyone from embarrassment." If you find yourself using any of these phrases, take note.

The real question to ask anytime you face the role of aggravator is this: *Am I putting others down in order to elevate myself or to elevate another person who deserves to be lifted up?*

You are also wise to ask yourself: *Have I aggravated anyone in the past? Do I need to ask forgiveness of someone I have aggravated?*

3. THE SPECTATOR WATCHES FROM A DISTANCE

The spectator watches from the sideline as others play the game of life. The spectator differs from the escapist in this way: the escapist doesn't even show up at the game or ignores the fact that there's a possible game to be played and won; the spectator knows there's a game—he has dreams of winning—but he never ventures out on the field.

The positive role of spectator is one we all should play from time to time. Not every person can play or win every game. We all need cheerleaders on the sideline. The father who applauds his daughter's piano recital performances, the mother who cheers on her daughter at a basketball game, the father who shows up and silently nods approval at all of his son's tennis matches, the mother who helps provide cupcakes for the class party in her child's honor . . . these are valuable and positive spectators.

The positive spectator steps aside so others can share or take the spotlight. The positive spectator sits down so others can stand up and speak. The positive spectator is the professional who gives the amateur a chance, the skilled mentor who allows his student a turn, the experienced performer who gives the newcomer a chance. The positive spectator is marked by an unselfish and generous spirit toward others.

The negative spectator, however, is usually bound by fear. It may be a fear of failure, a fear of rejection, a fear of calling attention to oneself. The negative spectator wants to play, and believes not only playing the game but winning the game is important or good, yet he chooses instead to sit on the sidelines and watch. The negative spectator can easily become frustrated or bitter, and all too often, negative spectators opt for becoming escapists.

A negative spectator plays the game for a while, and if success is not his immediately, or if he suffers what he perceives to be too hard a blow, he walks off the field and never returns to the game.

From personal experience I know what it means to be both

kinds of spectator. I know what it means to take a break and cheer for others. I also know what it means to be too scared to try to play.

I first met my best friend, Neil, in kindergarten, and throughout the many years of our friendship, he has always been an encourager in getting me to step off the sideline and onto the playing field.

One day in grade school, the boys decided to play softball, and I quickly retreated to the sideline. Knowing I could not hold a bat, Neil persuaded the other guys to let me play by having someone bat for me, and then if that person hit the ball, I would run the bases. As the guys picked their teammates, Neil convinced his team to pick me. Brian, the best player in our class, was also on our team.

Brian was an exceptional batter. He could hit the ball over the outfield players' heads, something few in our grade could do. Sometimes he even hit the side of the school building! When it was my turn to bat, Neil arranged for Brian to bat for me. As Brian corked the ball into left field time after time, I frantically ran the bases, and when Brian and I occasionally scored, the other team made no secret of their shock and disgust.

The first time our team took the field, however, I saw no recourse except to be a spectator. I headed for the bench as the other team members grabbed their gloves and ran out onto the field. Neil saw me sit down, came over, and asked, "What are you doing?"

"There's no use for me to stand out there and do nothing," I said.

"Johnny, you've got to play your outs just like everyone else. Get out there!" he replied.

I had no idea how I was going to play outfield, but I ran to the field where Neil pointed. As the innings passed, I discovered that I could stop the ball if it came my way and then kick it to a nearby player, who could throw it to the appropriate destination in the infield. At that grade level, not very many balls were hit, much less hit into the outfield, much less hit at the fly ball level where an outright catch of the ball might be expected. Neil didn't allow me to be a spectator, and I've never forgotten that.

I also learned in that first day on the baseball field an important lesson: sometimes you don't learn how to play the game until you are actually out on the field.

There's no way to fully anticipate all of the challenges any job or career or relationship might hold. Most of what we learn, we learn by doing and often in the heat of a crisis or in a have-to situation. If we wait until we have "enough" education or the "right" opportunity to get out onto the playing field, we'll probably remain on the sidelines forever.

Negative spectators usually must face the fact that it's not the game that's dangerous, difficult, or overly demanding; it's stepping out onto the playing field that is the big risk. Personal fear, far more than any aspect of the task, is the first and highest hurdle.

I have never been too scared to give a speech. That doesn't mean I am unacquainted with nervous jitters before walking out to speak to a first-time audience or an audience in which I know there are people I admire greatly. The speaking platform is my playing field, and before every "game," I have to make a choice to move from being a spectator backstage in the wings to being the person who steps behind the microphone.

I don't know what your "sport" may be but I do know this: it takes courage to play the game.

I also know that it takes endurance to stay in the game until you win.

Several years ago I felt a strong desire to meet new people, encounter new ideas, and take on a new challenge. I went back to college to work on a master's degree in social work. When I was an undergraduate, my major was communication, so this degree program represented a new academic field for me. It became a field that I found very exciting. In fact, I find it more and more exciting the longer I study and work in it.

Part of my degree program, which I completed in 1999, involved my working as a counselor in an internship setting. I discovered that I'm a good speaker, and a good listener.

I have also discovered that it takes a certain amount of courage and commitment to meet a new client and engage in a new long-term relationship with someone you genuinely hope to help. It's a different kind of courage from that needed to walk out on stage, but courage is required nonetheless.

One thing that happened as I pursued the advanced degree was that I needed to make adjustments in my speaking schedule to accommodate my grad-school schedule and internship hours. I became a positive spectator, to a degree, in taking some time away from the speaking circuit to study.

I came away from the experience with a strong belief that a retreat to the sideline can be a very good move for a person to make from time to time. On the sideline a spectator can often gain a new perspective on life or set new priorities. The sideline becomes a place for adjustment and refocus and renewal. In the end, what I learned while being a spectator has enhanced my work as a speaker.

The real question to ask if you find yourself in the role of a spectator is this: *Am I sitting on the sideline because I'm afraid to walk out onto the playing field of life, or am I sitting on the sideline to prepare myself more fully for the next time I take the field?*

4. THE PARTICIPATOR PLAYS TO WIN

The participator actively plays life's game—and not only plays *at* it, but *plays to win.*

I mentioned Neil in the previous section. He is definitely a participator in life, and like all positive participators I know, he encourages others to participate fully too. Actually he *demands it.*

For years, Neil and his wife have taken an annual ski vacation. They periodically invited me to go along, but for various reasons, I declined their kind invitations. Then came the year when I mentioned to Neil that I thought I'd like to try skiing someday. After that, well, it was all downhill. Neil wouldn't take "no" for an answer.

Neil was especially eager for me to try the new shoe skis— much shorter and more maneuverable than the more traditional skis and used without poles. With excitement and hesitation I agreed.

I suspect that most participators enter new challenges with both emotions at work. I certainly faced the possibility of failure, even injury. It's one thing to have a broken leg if you have two arms to help compensate for that injury. It's another thing to have a broken leg if you use your feet and toes as other people use their hands and fingers.

As hesitant as I was, I was also excited about the challenge, about a fun time with good friends, about the opportunity to soak up the beautiful scenery of the Colorado Rockies, about taking a break from an exhausting work schedule.

Did I fall? More times than I care to count.

Did I like falling? Absolutely not.

Did I have moments of fear? You bet. There were times when that mountain looked like a sheer vertical drop to me. Neil wasn't at all content with my skiing the bunny hill. He thought the instructors who were working with me were babying me. So he took over the instruction and insisted I ski a more advanced green run. I wanted to walk down the steep parts of that run but Neil demanded that I ski them.

Did I have embarrassing moments? Sure. Neil would insist when I fell, "Get up! You're embarrassing yourself!"

Did I love moments when the skis went in the direction I wanted them to go, and the tall evergreens created one of the most wonderful avenues I've ever traveled, and I slowly and perfectly navigated my way across the pristine snow? Yes, yes, yes.

Will I choose to participate again? Without a doubt!

Can there be such a thing as a negative participator? Absolutely. The negative participator can be a gang member—fully participating, just participating in the wrong things and for the wrong reasons. The negative participator can be the drug dealer who participates fully in a group that is crime oriented, the bigot who participates fully in isolating his group of friends from all others deemed "unworthy," the clique creator intent upon engineering her own social set, the person who disrupts positive meetings, events, or work. There are countless manifestations of negative participation—people who are fully involved and highly energetic in pursuing the wrong things.

One danger in being a participator is overparticipation. *Stressed out* and *burned out* are terms that readily come to mind! There are times and seasons for increased participation; there are also times to reduce involvement and allow a season for creative input.

The key questions to ask if you find yourself in the role of a participator are these: *Am I participating in something that is harmful or helpful? Am I helping others grow—materially, financially, emotionally, mentally, or spiritually?*

FOR EVERY SEASON AND SITUATION, A ROLE THAT'S RIGHT

Each of us has unique opportunities to play each of these roles at various times in our lives, and we shouldn't entirely avoid any of the roles. Each has a valid time and place. Finding a balance among the four roles is essential to a full and fulfilling life.

I struggle at times—as I am convinced all people do—at knowing which particular role to play in specific situations. Even as an adult, I find that when I visit my parents' home for a holiday weekend, life there is pretty much the same as it was when was growing up. My older brothers are a little slower athletically, but they still feel the call to the outdoors to shoot skeet, ride four-wheelers, or toss a football with their children. And I still sometimes find myself standing on the sideline watching. In those moments, I allow myself the joy of watching, knowing that at many of the events in which I am a participator, they are spectators.

What *is* important to me is taking the time and effort to make an evaluation of the role I am playing in any given setting. I ask myself these questions, which I encourage you to ask as you face various situations:

- Is this the role I truly *want* to take? Is my choice based upon an objective evaluation of the situation or emotions such as fear, jealousy, or revenge?

- Is this the role I should take for the good of all concerned—myself, my family, my associates, my friends? The best decision is always a win-win decision for all those who matter most to you.

- Is this a role that will move my life forward—perhaps not in the immediate short term but definitely in the long term? Are there ways in which my taking this role can provide genuine benefit to me or to someone close to me?

- Is this a role that provides a healthy challenge for me? Is it something worth my time, energy, and skills?

Simple and *easy* are two different things. Take the game of football—all a team has to do is get the ball from one end of the field to the other and prevent the opposing team from taking the ball away. Simple. But not easy. The same holds true for life. Many of the things we need to do are simple, and we discount them because they are simple. In truth, the simple things are sometimes the hardest things to do.

Seven

WHAT ARE YOUR CHANCES AT MAKING THE PLAY-OFFS?

DURING THE LAST HALF OF THE 1996 FOOTBALL season, the Miami Dolphins were on a losing streak. The players and even the coaches were showing signs of discouragement. Everyone involved—from the team owners to the fans—knew that if the Dolphins were to keep their play-off hopes alive, they needed to secure a win the next weekend in an important game against the formidable Indianapolis Colts.

The Dolphins' head coach, Jimmy Johnson, decided to address the problem at the Wednesday morning team meeting. He wanted the players to look past their 4-5 record and three straight losses. He later wrote about his plans for the meeting: "Instead of talking about how we'd beat Indianapolis, I thought it was more important [to deal with] self-inspection." He was determined to get them beyond feeling sorry for themselves.

At the meeting, Johnson reminded his players that even in the midst of hardship and limitations, they had options. He used the motto "Find a Way" to articulate the mind-set he hoped each man would adopt.

And then Johnson showed the Dolphins my video, *Armed with Hope*. This twenty-five-minute video was produced while I was a full-time employee with the Ziglar Corporation. The message is a simple one: "If you don't have the best of everything, make the most of everything you have." The video shows how I deal with some of life's practical details, from using a computer to carrying luggage. Johnson later wrote to me:

> The entire team was moved when I played them your video. It showed, in a way far better than anything I could have said, that it is possible to "Find a Way" to deal with whatever challenges we might face.

Game day arrived. The Dolphins started off slowly with a severe lack of offensive drive. The team was down 3-0 when Olindo Mare nailed a field goal. Then Miami seemed to energize itself dramatically after the team got its hands on an Indy punt. Dan Marino capitalized on the team's burst of renewed energy and hit O. J. McDuffie with a thirty-six-yard touchdown pass.

Miami went on to win 37-13. On the way to the victory, Marino set two amazing records: he became the first quarterback to throw for fifty thousand yards, and he became the first quarterback to complete four thousand passes.

In his letter to me, Johnson wrote,

> Our team took that message [*Armed with Hope*] to heart and played one of their best games of the season. Our theme of finding a way, which was made so clear by your video, was reinforced

all week in our meetings and our practices, and helped pave the way to an outstanding performance on game day.

I felt honored that my story had helped generate a success.

Finding a way is really the goal we all face—not just in the long-range context of our lives, but in our daily struggles and decisionmaking.

Finding a way is proactive—it isn't stumbling across a way or lashing out to create a path through the forest. It means taking a look at options and then making choices.

Finding a way is a challenge that requires a certain amount of objectivity about our lives.

THE LIGHT OF OBJECTIVITY

When a condition such as job loss, illness, or marriage conflict flares up, we experience intense feelings that can impair our judgment and cause us to lose our way. Feelings such as fear and anger kick in and cause us to lose sight of our options and make rash decisions. Those are the times we become our own worst enemies.

We may say to ourselves: "I'm no good at that." "The timing is bad." "Those people don't understand." Recognize these statements as an attempt to deny the problem, laugh it off, or blame it on someone or something else. Psychologists call this run away type of reaction "flight."

Or we might get mad and react by haphazardly attacking the problem with full energy. We stress ourselves out by trying harder and working longer. Unfortunately, such forceful efforts can leave us feeling as though we've been running around in circles or banging our heads against the proverbial wall. If we're not careful we can get drawn deeper into the problem. Some-times the harder we try, the more frustrated we become. Psychologists call this stand-firm type of reaction "fight."

But, there is a better choice that can help us find a way: allowing the light of objectivity to shine on your situation.

Obviously, the word *objectivity* derives from the word *object*. The origin of *object* comes from a postclassical meaning of the Latin *objectum*, which means, "something put in someone's way so that it can be seen." Too often we get so bogged down in limitations and frustrations that we can't see a situation plainly. But, when we take a step back and look at the condition with some objectivity we see it more clearly. We become free—free to take a nonthreatening and honest look at ourselves, listen to others' suggestions, and recognize options that we may have previously overlooked. The light of objectivity exposes the big picture of your life.

BE OBJECTIVE ABOUT THE TOTAL CONTEXT OF YOUR LIFE

Perhaps because I have studied art and enjoy painting, I am keenly aware that context dramatically shapes perspective. The size, color, and mass of a frame highlight certain colors and details in a piece of artwork, even as these factors diminish other aspects of the work. A gold frame will emphasize the hues and tones of light in a painting, but a black frame on the same work will draw attention to the lines and shadows. Context always influences what we experience as content in any given situation.

That principle also holds true for life. People and places—our family members, friends, church affiliations, office settings,

John painting.

homes, communities all influence who we are and how we live.

When my big-city friends come to visit me at my home in Breese, they are often surprised to discover that the residents of my small hometown often leave their doors unlocked and the keys in their cars while running into a store. We who live in Breese have a feeling of safety that many people don't have, perhaps because we know one another well, and as a result, we also know when a stranger comes to town. That's part of the context in which I live.

I also live in the context of my family heritage.

Foppe isn't a particularly common name, except in the area where I live in Clinton County, Illinois. Foppes have lived in Clinton County for more than 160 years. Not only do I have brothers and a father in various enterprises in southern Illinois, but a number of close and distant cousins proudly have put the family name on their business establishments.

Several years ago, I was required to do a genealogy project as part of my social work degree, and in the process, I became keenly interested in my family history. As part of studying my family roots, I made a trip to Germany. My parents had also become interested in knowing more about our ancestors, and my father made the trip with me.

I'll never forget the day when we actually set foot on the "family farm" in Germany, the one that my great-great-great-grandfather Bernard Anton left as he embarked on a new life in America. There was a sense of familiarity, of being home. That sense was heightened as I looked into the faces of my distant relatives and they looked into my face. They could see in me and in my father the features of family members they knew well. I found that I had deep empathy with the message of the proverb that was inscribed at the entrance to the Foppe farm:

> What you can do today,
> don't postpone until tomorrow.
> Because your God and Master will take
> care of tomorrow.
> Today is still your day.
> Who knows if you are still here
> tomorrow.

This is a translation from the original German inscription:

Was Du heute tun und verrichten kannst verschiebe nicht auf morgen Denn fuer morgen wird Dein herr und Gott schon sorgen. Heut ist noch Deine frist were weiss ob Du morgen noch bist.

I discovered on that trip that I have a great deal of German in me. I am a product not simply of Dad and Mom, but of generations before them. I am a product of my family. They are the ones from whom I have acquired my strong work ethic, my values, my ambition. As I have studied my ancestors, I see repeated traits:

- determination
- practicality
- entrepreneurship
- critical thinking
- unwillingness to settle for less than the best
- faith

I do not exist in a vacuum. I did not create myself. There's much to be said for exploring one's roots and for analyzing one's family ties. I have often said, "My family is my greatest strength and my greatest weakness." Having a loving family means that I don't always push myself as hard as I might. Having a strong family means that I have support when I collapse from pushing myself too hard.

AN OBJECTIVE LOOK AT YOUR FEELINGS

You need to become an objective observer of your life, especially of your feelings and the way you express them.

Is it possible to analyze your feelings? Absolutely. It's a worthy exercise for every person to take time occasionally to ask, *How am I feeling right now? Have I been feeling this way very long? Is this emotion a deeply entrenched pattern of response in my life?* Are you

- angry?
- lonely?
- frustrated?
- overwhelmed?
- bored?

- emotionally exhausted?
- rejected?
- content?
- enthusiastic?
- determined?
- hopeful?

The first step in dealing objectively with feelings is pinpointing as closely as possible the exact nature of a particular feeling or mix of feelings. Emotions tend to cluster, and clusters of emotions tend to form patterns. Emotional exhaustion and frustration often go together. Feelings of being overwhelmed and of being rejected often seem to link up with feelings of anger.

Singular emotions are usually recognized rather easily. It's when emotions compound and grow, or you allow your emotions to take on the characteristics of a pattern, that you may need help from someone you trust. Objectivity results not from shutting out feelings but from becoming aware of them so you can change them. You must first feel and then deal with what you feel.

I like the approach John Powell outlines in *Through the Seasons of the Heart* for personally handling feelings in a healthy way:

We allow our emotions to arise so that they can be identified. We observe the patterns in our emotional reactions, report them and judge them. Having done these things, we instinctively and immediately make the necessary adjustments in the light of our own ideals and hopes for growth. We change.

Allow yourself to feel. Don't try to shut down or shut off emotional responses to life. You were made with emotions, and the expression of them is valuable.

Identify what you are feeling, and observe the patterns of your feelings.

And then make adjustments in the light of your "own ideals and hopes for growth." Ah, therein lies the crux of the issue for many people. They don't know their own ideals. They don't have hopes for growth—at least not ideals that they are deeply committed to pursuing.

If you are struggling emotionally or are feeling pain, I heartily recommend that you take a long, hard look at what you believe to be true and valuable and worthy. What *are* the traits or qualities you value most in your life? What are the behaviors that cause you to feel respect, admiration, or a desire to emulate? What are the hopes you hold for your own life and your future? Who do you want to *be* . . . who do you want to *become*?

AN OBJECTIVE LOOK AT
YOUR BEHAVIORAL RESPONSES

All emotions are valid. Not all *behaviors* that arise from emotions are good, however.

As a young person, I often thought that if I kept my feelings in check, I could somehow separate my feelings from a tense situation and keep myself safe. As I have matured, I have come to recognize that it's not my emotions that I need to keep in check, but the ways in which I *express* my emotions. My behavior needs to be tempered, adjusted, altered, modified. My responses to my emotions and my responses to others in the wake of my emotions need to be objectively analyzed in the light of what I hold to be values that are worthy.

It is in choosing how you will behave that you need an extra dose of objectivity. Here are six practical suggestions for behaving in an objective manner that is not swayed by emotional mood swings or intense emotional reactions:

1. Give Yourself Time and Distance

Put some time and distance between your emotional response to a situation and any behavioral response. For example: You're in a job setting where your boss is disrespectful, or you're not being treated fairly, and you'd like to walk out. Allow yourself to cool down before making a rash decision like quitting. Try to sleep on the problem, decision, or opportunity. A good night's sleep often yields clarity. Take a few days to mull over a key decision. Consider how you felt when you first heard about the need for the decision and how you have felt as hours and days have passed. Outline various approaches you might take in acting on the situation. Permit your alternatives to gel in your mind and heart for a while.

2. Examine Your Beliefs

Ask yourself how your core beliefs relate to the situation you are facing and the response you believe you should make to the situation.

I was recently inspired by a story about one of my high-school classmates and his wife, Matt and Erica. The young couple are striving to make their marriage survive in the midst of tremendous adversity by adhering to their beliefs about marriage.

A couple of years ago, Erica was diagnosed with Hodgkin's lymphoma. As she underwent two surgeries and six months of chemotherapy, Matt stuck by her side. Thankfully, Erica's cancer is now in remission. But a few months ago, tragedy struck again. Matt broke his neck in a car accident, and he is paralyzed from the shoulders down.

Now it's Erica's turn to stick by her husband's side as he undergoes intense daily physical therapy. You've heard of "for better or for worse, in sickness and in health"?

"We're going on seven years of marriage and we're testing all of the vows," Erica says. With their love for each other and their beliefs as guideposts, Matt and Erica are forging ahead—together!

Are your emotions in concert with the behavior you intend to display? Does your behavior contradict what you truly believe to be significant, valuable, or honorable?

3. Identify the Facts

Focus on what you know. Refuse to speculate or to play what-if games. If you've ever been on jury duty, you know that our criminal justice system in America strives to administer justice based on the facts of a case. As a juror you quickly learn that you are not supposed to allow hearsay, rumors, media spin, prejudices, or strictly circumstantial evidence to sway your verdict.

Concentrate on the known factors: who, what, when, where, how, expressed intent as to why. Take a look at what people actually said or wrote, without reading motive into the words.

4. Challenge Your Assumptions

Challenging our assumptions frees us from looking at life from only one perspective and helps us distinguish reality from an illusion. A friend of mine recently visited the Louvre Art Museum in Paris. When he spotted one of his favorite works of art—the famous painting of *Whistler's Mother,* he got excited, turned to a friend who was accompanying him, and said, "Look, they have copy of *Whistler's Mother* here!" His companion laughed and declared, "That IS *Whistler's Mother!*" My friend knew that James Whistler was born in America and just assumed that the picture he saw was a reproduction. His ethnocentric assumption made him miss the obvious beauty right before him.

In order to challenge your assumptions, recognize that appearances—real or imagined—can be deceiving. Play the devil's advocate with yourself, and consider different perspectives. Weigh possible reasons another person might have for his actions.

5. Gain Insight from Others

Seek out two of three people whom you respect and know will be honest with you. Ask their opinions. I caution you to limit the opinions you solicit—too many viewpoints and you'll only end up confused. Avail yourself of the wisdom of others, preferably those who hold like values and who have personal experience with the issue you are facing. Whenever I am pondering an important business decision or struggling to put a speech together, I seek out insight from my mentor, Zig Ziglar. Search for mentors or people who will work with you to help you maximize your potential—not people who will discourage you from trying.

6. Be Open to Consulting a Professional

Getting help in any situation—emotional, marital, family, or financial—is not a sign of weakness or ignorance. It is a sign of strength and openness. Countless people have found peace of mind and preserved important relationships because they had the courage to talk with a therapist.

If you have never consulted a professional about your goals, dreams, or problems, I encourage you to do so. The money you spend on a professional's fee may save you time and heartache in the long run. Once I was trying to decorate a large room in my house. The existing wallpaper looked dull, and I was prepared to enlist a lot of help from my brothers to strip the paper and re-decorate the room. If you've ever stripped wallpaper, you know that it can be a grueling and messy task. Fortunately I hired an interior decorator who advised me to simply put a decorative wallpaper border over the existing paper. In a matter of minutes, we transformed the entire appearance of the room and saved ourselves a lot of hard work and money. Now, it's one of my favorite rooms in the house thanks to her professional advice.

Nobody can be totally objective about his life, his needs, or his potential. Neither can a person know all there is to know about any particular situation, challenge, opportunity, or decision. Avail yourself of the skills and expertise of others who are well trained.

Genuine objectivity nearly always produces options. Once you recognize and define options, you can set goals. Once you set goals, you can make plans. Once you make plans, you can implement them with more focus and precision, effective-ness, and productivity. Success becomes reachable.

Don't ignore the total context of your life.

Don't hide from your emotions.

Don't try to duck responsibility for your behavior.

Face all three.

An objective look at the whole of your life can help you find a way.

$\mathcal{W}$e come from God and we

go back to God. Our lives are in

His hands. We are worthy

because He says we are worthy.

Eight

HOW BIG A LIFE ARE YOU WILLING TO PURSUE?

AT AGE THREE, SHORTLY AFTER I WAS FITTED WITH prosthetic hooks, I was chosen to throw out the first ball at a Shriners benefit baseball game at Busch Stadium in St. Louis. I met all the players in the locker room before the game. One of the most famous Cardinals of all time, Lou Brock, asked me how far I was going to throw the ball, and I proudly announced, "Out of the stadium!"

That has pretty much been my attitude all of my life. I may not be able to do everything but then again, who can? For that matter, who really wants to be able to do everything or have to do everything?

I am committed to doing everything I choose to do to the very best of my ability.

WHAT YOU EXPECT FROM YOURSELF COUNTS THE MOST

I meet countless people as I travel here in the United States and overseas who are seeking to live up to the expectations that others have held or continue to hold for them. Although it is a wonderful thing to have people who believe in you and believe in all that you can be, it is a terrible burden to have others relying upon you to fulfill their dreams for you. In many cases, these people are actually relying upon you to fulfill the dreams they once had for themselves.

The truth is, apart from your Creator, nobody can ever know you as well as you can know yourself.

There is nothing to be gained from rebellion just for the sake of rebellion against what others recognize to be your strengths and abilities. To forge a path that may be wrong for you simply because you don't want to pursue what a father, mother, or teacher thinks is right is foolish. If others hold a strong opinion about your talents and abilities, take another look at yourself. Are they right? Do you, indeed, have that talent or ability? Do you have that quality, trait, or strength? If so, find a way that is right for you to develop that ability.

You may or may not be an enthusiastic fan of Yoko Ono, the widow of John Lennon, but it is an interesting fact of her life that her parents believed strongly in her ability to be a good artist. They encouraged her to pursue her artistic ability and made arrangements for her to study, travel, and train as an artist.

Her parents hoped that she would pursue a classical career in art. They saw her as a fine artist in the traditional, more realistic mode.

Yoko Ono's art is anything but traditional, realistic, or classical. She has marched to the beat of a far different drummer. However, she is an artist. What her parents saw in her was valid. Her expression of her talent is her own.

So, too, with you.

Others may have an accurate take on your innate abilities, your positive personality traits, and even your God-given purpose on this earth. They can never fully predict, however, your unique expression of your abilities and personality, or the way in which God might lead you to fulfill your purpose. The fulfillment of your purpose must be *your* project, and it is therefore subject to your motivation.

Just as you should never rely on others to define your potential, never expect others to provide a motivation for you to reach that potential. Others may encourage you. It's a marvelous thing to have encouragers and those who applaud your successes. It's a great thing to have others believe in you to succeed and to root for you. Yet you should never rely on others for constant encouragement, applause, or rousing cheers of support.

Ultimately it's up to you to find your source of inner motivation to pursue your dreams. You must come up with your own expectations for yourself and then work hard to turn those expectations into accomplishments. Lead *yourself*.

YOU SET THE TONE FOR HOW YOU WILL BE RESPECTED

I learned recently that the old song made famous by Aretha Franklin, "R-E-S-P-E-C-T," has been named one of the top five songs of the 20th century. I certainly agree with the song's message!

The Bible tells us to love our neighbors as we love ourselves. Unless you have respect for your integrity and uniqueness as a human being, you can't really love another person. I know I have to take care of myself and meet my needs so I am able to give of myself more fully to others.

In the early days of my public speaking, I spoke mostly to youth groups on topics generally related to self-esteem and establishing a positive self-image. I thought that as I grew older, there would be less need to address these issues. I was wrong. Just as many people today seem to suffer from poor self-esteem as when I began speaking nearly fifteen years ago.

Jack Canfield is the founder and CEO of the Foundation for Self-Esteem but is perhaps better known for his role as coauthor of the *Chicken Soup for the Soul* books. Jack once defined *self-esteem* as "the willingness to participate in life with a sense of oneself as a worthwhile person." I like that definition. And by that definition, I have healthy self-esteem. I am willing to participate as fully as possible in life, and I have no doubt that I am a worthwhile person!

I was asked to submit a press kit to an organization of handicapped people so they might consider having me speak to a chapter meeting of their group. I soon received a reply that went something like this: "Thanks for sending your material. We don't think you're right for our group. You have overcome most of life's obstacles through your own effort, while the members of our group can't function independently and need the support of others. Most of our meetings are focused on ways in which we can raise public awareness of the plight of the handicapped and gain additional support."

I simply didn't fit their profile of what a "handicapped" person should be and do. More important, I didn't fit their expectation that a handicapped person should *need* and *expect* help from others rather than seek to be as independent as possible.

Trust me. I didn't think I was a good fit for their group either. Many people with unique physical conditions may need more help than I need. But I am also aware that a sizable percentage of people with conditions have given up doing all they can personally do, and they choose instead to *expect* others to assist them.

I want nothing to do with pity. It only drags a person down to a level of lower self-expectations and lower self-worth.

I don't allow others to dictate my feelings of respect, dignity, or worth. I take responsibility for myself in these areas. I am the one who determines whether I have self-respect or self-worth or personal dignity.

If others are uncomfortable with my condition, I take responsibility for finding people who are supportive of me and comfortable being around me—and then I nurture these relationships.

I take responsibility for my education and training. Through the years I have been amazed at the number of people who register surprise that I have a baccalaureate degree—with honors, I hasten to add—and a master's degree. I wouldn't have expected anything less from myself. I am deeply committed to a lifetime of learning. I know it's my responsibility to study continually if I want to stay at the top of any field I choose to pursue.

I take responsibility for my income. I work hard at being a successful entrepreneur. I am not at all comfortable with the idea of letting the government support me. I learned early in life that when others help you, they also require certain things of you. There's always a payback of some kind. I'd rather do my utmost always to remain self-sufficient financially and be the captain of my own ship.

I take responsibility for my emotional health. Sure, I am skeptical at times. I can be skeptical when I consider my dating situation and wonder whether I am ever going to find the right girl, or when I think about losing some of my flexibility as I enter old age. Sure, I feel stress at times. I get frustrated when I can't seem to master bagging my own groceries, using the self-serve soft-drink dispensers at McDonald's, or pointing out something to my assistant on her computer screen.

Yes, frustration and stress threaten my emotional stability at times, but I know I am not alone in that. These enemies of emotional health have nothing to do with my lack of arms. It's up to me to decide to wake up with a positive attitude, and it's up to me to maintain that attitude, regardless of what may happen to me on any given day or in any given circumstance. It's up to me to take time out to engage in healthful recreation and relaxation, and to learn to let go of some worries and frustrations that contribute to stress.

I take responsibility for my spiritual health. It's up to me to accept God's love for me and to accept His forgiveness and to forgive myself. It's up to me to seek out and then fulfill His mission for my life. It's up to me to deal with the natural doubts and fears that try to dent my faith. It's up to me to set aside time each day to pray, sit in quiet reflection, and read inspirational materials.

It's up to me to value my own dreams to the point that I will actually pursue them.

YOU SET THE STANDARDS
FOR HOW GOOD YOU WANT TO BE

Achievement requires focus, discipline, and practice. You, and you alone, determine how much discipline and practice you want to commit to the pursuit of any goal.

While I am deeply committed to becoming all that I can become as a person, I am not a believer in perfection. We seem to demand perfection in our culture. It's an ideal we can never attain, and it's likely the cause of much stress in our world. I certainly don't have the societal idea of a perfect body, and I never will. There's a difference between striving for the best body I *can* have and perfection. There's always a difference between seeking to attain quality and striving for perfection.

Striving for what cannot be obtained brings pain. We need to set standards of excellence for our lives that are within reach—perhaps a stretch, but nevertheless, within reach.

In the end, it's the standard of excellence you set for your life that will determine how much time and effort you want to invest in achieving any goal. Don't let anyone else set that standard for you. Live up to your standards of excellence.

Does this mean that I dismiss moral and ethical excellence? Not at all. I hope that you will set very high standards for your moral and ethical behavior, and that you will make the development of character your foremost goal. In setting that goal for yourself, however, you will find a commitment and an ongoing motivation for reaching your goal. If others tell you to be good, you'll probably rebel or perhaps berate yourself for failing to be good in the face of every temptation. If you determine within yourself that you are going to work at your character development with God's help, you are likely to succeed in mastering the art of good living.

Once you have established your standards regarding values and character, refuse to compromise to a lower standard.

I had a friend in high school who felt that the only way she could get guys to like her was to have sex with them. She slept with every guy who expressed an interest in her. She went through boyfriends faster than most of us went through acne medicine.

Then came the day when she thought she was pregnant. She sought out my counsel, and I helped her the best I could. At the same time, I referred her to professional counseling and to a good doctor. Fortunately for her sake, she was not pregnant. But then she confided that she had really hoped she *was* pregnant because she thought a baby would help her hold on to a boyfriend and give her a purpose for living.

I didn't have all of life's answers at that time and still don't, but I knew even then that when a person compromises her moral values and sullies her own character simply to manipulate other people, something is wrong.

Little did I realize then that countless people behave in a similar way every day. They justify their compromises in moral standards by looking at what they hope will be the end result: the manipulation of others to do their bidding or to satisfy their needs. It might be a little lie here, a little dishonesty there, a manufactured crisis, an overstatement of a problem. They are looking for sympathy, expressions of support and understanding, and sometimes outright reward.

Bad means can't lead to good ends.

There's another way to live!

THE FIRST PLACE TO LOOK FOR ACCOUNTABLITY

The first place to look for accountability is in your mirror. Just as you set your standards for self-worth, respect, and character excellence, you are responsible for your pursuit of these standards. You must answer to yourself for every success and failure.

I keep the following poem taped to my bathroom mirror:

THE GUY IN THE GLASS

When you get what you want in your struggle for pelf
And the world makes you king for a day
Just go to a mirror and look at yourself,
And see what THAT guy has to say.

For it isn't your Father or Mother or Wife
Whose judgment upon you must pass;
The feller whose verdict counts most in your life
Is the one staring back from the glass.

He's the feller to please, never mind all the rest
For he's with you clear up to the end,
And you've passed your most dangerous, difficult test
If the guy in the glass is your friend.

You may be like Jack Horner and "chisel" a plum,
And think you're wonderful guy,
But the man in the glass says you're only a bum
If you can't look him straight in the eye.

You may fool the whole world down the pathway of years
And get pats on the back as you pass
But your final reward will be heartaches and tears
If you've cheated the guy in the glass.

—COPYRIGHT DALE WIMBROW, © 1934

THE ROOT OF ALL DIGNITY

I don't buy into the idea that we need to acquire skills or develop an ability in order to obtain self-worth. Self-worth is not the sum of what we do. One sleepless night I was praying and I came to this conclusion: if we allow our "doing" to determine our "being," then we are in danger of being outdone at every turn. Our self-worth is in a constant state of fluctuation depending on our latest achievement or failure.

Rather than base my self-worth on what I do, I have chosen as my basis for self-worth this fact: I am a son of God. That's the only consistent, lasting basis for self-esteem. We come from God, and we go back to God. Our lives are in His hands. We are worthy because He says we are worthy. He thought we were worthy to be born, He thinks we are worthy to live, and He has made the provision of His forgiveness available to us because He thinks we are worthy to live forever.

How much are you willing to trust God?

As I have already related and as you perhaps can well imagine, my birth sent shock waves of fear through my entire family. When one of my grandmothers heard the news that I had no arms, and then heard the news that I needed to have an operation to connect my upper and lower colon, she responded in a blunt but honest way, "Let's just pray that the good Lord takes the baby."

My father responded, "No, that would be asking for the easy way out. We have to pray for God's will." My grandmother was stunned to hear such courageous words of wisdom coming from her young son-in-law.

My father was willing to trust God not only with the ongoing existence of my life, but also with the outcome of my life.

Much of our self-esteem rests in how much we are willing to turn our lives over to God for *His* making of us. I like what Mother Teresa once said: "Let Jesus use you without consulting you. We let Him take what He wants from us. So take whatever He gives and give whatever He takes with a big smile."

SO LET ME ASK YOU

Are you expecting big things from yourself? Have you set high standards of personal excellence?

Do you have a deep respect for yourself and for the One who made you?

Have you determined the level of character excellence you hope to achieve in your life?

Are you trusting God with your life?

Your answers to these questions will determine to a great extent how big a life you will live.

None of us can ever know
fully what it is like to live out
another person's life. Our
challenge is to figure out how to
live out our own lives fully!

Nine

HAVE YOU LAUGHED AT YOURSELF LATELY?

SHORTLY AFTER MY FRIEND NEIL AND I GRADUATED from college, I was asked to speak to a ready-mix concrete association meeting in Palm Springs, California. Neil and I thought the trip would give us a little break before we settled into jobs. The sunny, mild climate of Palm Springs in the early spring provided a wonderful setting for us. What twenty-one-year-old wouldn't enjoy a few days lounging by a pool or playing eighteen holes of golf on a lush course? In my case, of course, that golf game amounted to driving a golf cart.

I didn't know much about Palm Springs before I traveled there, other than the fact that it was a desirable desert vacation spot. I didn't know that the city rested at the foot of the San Bernardino Mountains, or that a daily sprinkling of rain was normal at that time of year. The misty cloud cover usually rolled in late in the afternoon, released its moisture, and then floated away.

On the second afternoon of our vacation, Neil and I were relaxing by the pool and getting more burned than tanned when the rain began. We quickly gathered our belongings and headed for our hotel room. On the way, Neil said, "I feel like getting out of here for a while. Do you want to go for a drive?"

That sounded like a great idea to me.

Back in our room, I changed out of my damp swim trunks into a dry jogging suit and tennis shoes. Neil threw a tank top over his swim trunks and slipped on some sandals.

We drove away from the hotel without a specific destination in mind. Since we were not on a particular schedule, we wandered aimlessly for a while until we found ourselves on the outskirts of the city. Neil noticed a billboard advertising the Palm Springs Aerial Tramway, a cable car ride up Mount San Jacinto. Neil asked me if I wanted to check it out, and I said, "Sure, why not?"

Neil turned off the highway and followed the road up to the foot of the mountain. We soon came to the terminal building. It appeared empty, and it was difficult to tell whether the tram was running. Just as we entered the lobby, however, a cable car descended through the low clouds and docked at the station. No one else was around. Neil enthusiastically said, "Let's go for a ride!" We bought our tickets, boarded the car, sat down, and waited. While we waited, we got into a deep conversation and were completely oblivious to everything around us. We paid no attention to the time or to anyone boarding the car.

At one point I overheard some kids softly snickering, but I dismissed their laughter and kept talking to Neil. Then one of the kids let out a loud giggle that caught Neil's attention. He glanced over his shoulder and thought, *Stupid kids.* He turned back to me to resume our conversation, and then suddenly he jerked his head around to take a second look at the kids. A puzzled expression came over his face. I asked him, "What's going on?" He didn't respond so I turned and looked

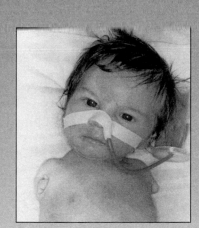

John in the hospital the first
or second day after his birth

Family photo with John shortly
after his birth: left to right, front
row: brother Tom, John, brother
Joe. Back row: brother Bill,
Carole (John's mother), and Ron
(John's father)

John writing on a
blackboard in the kitchen
with his toes

John wearing prosthetic hooks and
playing with his brothers Tom
(left) and Joe (right)

John with Dr. Herald Wilke, a minister who
was born without arms

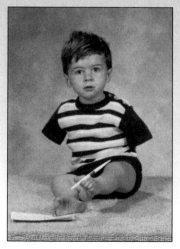

John holding a pen with
his toes

John playing the trombone using
his prosthetic arms and feet, age 9

Pope Paul VI blessing John
with a kiss in 1976

Photo by Jim Kennett

John, senior high
school photo, age 17

John playing "Rock, paper, scissors"
with his friends at the prom

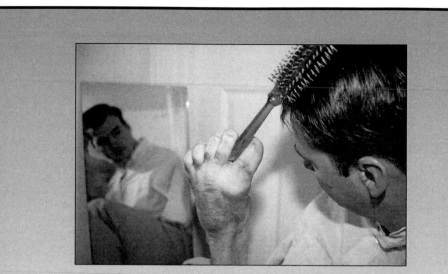

John combing his hair

John driving

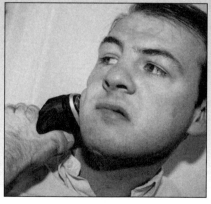

John shaving

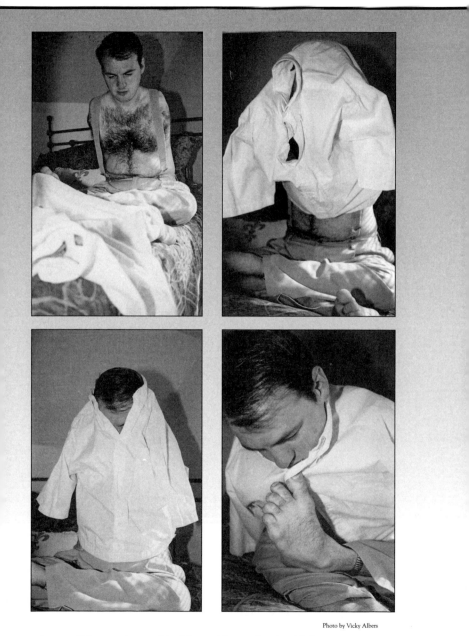

John putting on his shirt and buttoning it with his toes

John sitting poolside putting his
watch on his ankle

John at a speaking engagement

John speaking to
a group in Ohio

John pouring a drink with
his feet during a
presentation in Ohio

John and all his brothers. Left to right and youngest to oldest:
Paul, Patrick, Jim, Ron, John, Tom, Joe, and Bill

John giving a painting lesson to kids at a day-care center

also. The two kids who were giggling were sitting on a bench. They were dressed in heavy winter clothing, and one boy was holding a sled.

I looked at Neil in his swim trunks. He looked at me and then back at the kids. The adults with the children were dressed in snowsuits, with scarves and caps. Neil leaned to the edge of his seat to peer out the window as he asked in panic, "How high does this thing go? Is it cold up there?"

Just as he asked those questions, a man boarded the car and said, "What did you think? There's a beach up there?"

Neil not only looked stupid in that moment, he felt stupid. We had no time to react, however, to the predicament in which we had plunged ourselves. No sooner had we realized our error than the cable car door slammed shut and locked from the outside. The car began to float upward out of the docking area. Everyone on board found it hilarious that Neil was dressed so sparsely for the excursion to the top of a snow-capped mountain.

Since clouds had kept us from seeing the top of the mountain, we had no idea about the height of the peak. We had never stopped to ask, "How far does the tram go up?" It was only later that we learned that the elevation at the top of the mountain was 8,516 feet. It was only later that we learned that the Palm Springs Aerial Tramway has the steepest vertical cable rise in the United States and the second in the world!

There was nothing for me to do in that moment except shake my head and laugh. All of those people must have thought my best friend was a stereotypical blond surfer dude who didn't have a clue in life. They were wrong, but in that moment, it was easy to be wrong.

As the car slowly climbed upward, the air got colder and colder. By the time the car reached the second of the five towers that held the cables, we could see our breath inside the car cabin. I was cold, but at least I had on a jogging suit and shoes that gave me more protection than Neil's swim trunks, tank top, and sandals.

The other passengers tried to be polite but couldn't help smiling. The colder the air became, the funnier Neil's situation became. He began to shiver. He tried to act tough, as though the chill weren't affecting him, but I knew otherwise because he became very quiet—not at all his usual demeanor.

About halfway up, we caught a glimpse of the terrain below through the clouds. Tall pine trees seemed to reach off the cliff side in an attempt to brush the underside of the car. We could see a light dusting of snow on the ground below. The higher we rose, the more that dusting of snow turned into a blanket of snow. After about fifteen minutes, we finally docked at the top, and the cable car door popped open. The air hit us with a blast. Neil turned a pale shade of blue. We had no choice but to exit the car.

The kids with the sled raced out of the car with delight. We hesitated, then jumped out onto the snow. Neil jumped around a bit. It was too uncomfortable to stand in one place for more than a second. We ran over to the back side of the upper terminal building. Sure enough, a small ski area ran down the other side of the mountain. More people stopped to stare at Neil and murmured among themselves. A group of Japanese tourists openly giggled, and then one of the tourists reached for his camera and snapped a photograph of Neil.

At that point, Neil was fed up. He was irritated at both the cold and the embarrassment of looking so out of place. He paused only to form a snowball and hurl it over a cliff. Then we hurried back to the terminal to catch the next car down the mountain. We were the only two people on board for the return trip.

As the car descended through the cloud cover, the temperature warmed. Neil's shivering gradually subsided. Just before we reached the docking station, my best friend turned to me and said something I have never forgotten. "You know, John, up there, people didn't even notice that you didn't have arms! I was the strange one. Now I realize how tough life is for you."

I wish I could have bottled those words. Neil's comment deeply touched me because I knew it took a lot of courage for him to express such a tender sentiment of compassion.

The greater truth is that no one really knows fully what it is like to live out another person's life. We don't know the

Photo by Jim Kennett

John breaking eggs for breakfast.

exact extent, nature, or severity of his pain, hurts, struggles, or condition.

In our growing-up years, my brothers would sometimes try to imitate me and the way I use my toes. I took significant satisfaction in the fact that they were not at all adept at using their toes to hold a pencil or crayon, and they couldn't handle a fork or spoon or break eggs as well as I could. Unless you've seriously tried to live another person's life, you can't fully understand all that is required in overcoming his personal condition, external or internal.

But you can know that every person at some time in life has experienced pain or embarrassment, is experiencing pain or embarrassment, or will experience pain or embarrassment.

Every person at some time in life will feel rejection or alienation or prejudice for some reason.

Every person at some time in life will wish his life were different in some way.

Awkward, embarrassing, out-of-place moments are the fate of everyone.

A FOURFOLD RESPONSE

What can your response be?

First, you can be more alert and sensitive to the fact that others may be experiencing pain, sorrow, or loneliness.

Second, you can choose to express compassion to people whom you know are struggling. That takes courage, but it's the right thing to do.

Third, you can choose to take your lead from the other person about how to express your compassion and when to laugh along with him.

Fourth, you can develop a good sense of humor about yourself. You can learn to laugh in the midst of your struggle. I probably have one of the most extensive repertoires of jokes about not having any arms of any person in the nation.

LAUGHTER DEFUSES
EMBARRASSMENT AND TENSION

My friends and I were practicing a Christmas pageant in the gym at school one year. The lights were turned out to begin the program, and as we were all plunged into darkness, one of my friends said, "John, keep your hands to yourself." My friends all laughed but I probably laughed hardest of all.

Through my younger years some of my friends would tie the arms of my long-sleeved shirts to my desk or use the sleeves to gag my mouth. I knew they were engaging in the typical pranks of friendship, so I didn't mind.

A neighbor recently told me that some of the seniors at the local high school had sent the freshman class on a scavenger hunt. The tenth directive of the hunt: get the fingerprints of John Foppe. When my neighbor shared this bit of news with me, she was upset that her son had helped create this scavenger hunt, but I laughed!

A woman in a nursing home, who had just had a leg amputated, said to me as I visited her on a hospice call, "Did they cut you up too?" She was sadly serious, but I laughed.

When little children come to my door on Halloween, I always manage to open the door and, using my toes, reach into my cache of candy and place some in each sack held out to me. One mother related to me that her son returned from his trip to my front door with the exclamation, "Mom, you should see this guy's costume!" My response? I laughed.

When I first went to the Department of Motor Vehicles to see if there were any restrictions to be placed on my driver's license, I kept a straight face as I told the woman behind the counter that I thought I should only be allowed to drive a car that had an AM/FM stereo radio and cassette player. I laugh just remembering the look on her face!

When I fell down the slope of a muddy riverbank and had to call to friends to help me, I laughed. Well, later I laughed!

A plain and simple fact of life is this: if you laugh, you give others the freedom to laugh. And if they are allowed to laugh with you about any condition, they are not going to pity your condition or think less of you.

Laughter is the best way of defusing embarrassment.

Laughter is the best way to make friends.

Laughter is the best way to get through a difficult or awkward situation. It relieves stress and puts life into perspective.

Laughing at ourselves works to our good on many different levels. Try it!

Frequently, we are restlessly looking for answers, going from door to door, from book to book, or from school to school, without having really listened carefully and attentively to the questions . . . This is a very difficult task, because in our world we are constantly pulled away from our innermost self and encouraged to look for answers instead of listening to the questions.

—HENRI NOUWEN, REACHING OUT

Ten

ARE YOU ASKING THE RIGHT QUESTIONS?

AFTER MY BIRTH, MY PARENTS FACED AN INITIAL question: "Why was John born this way?" They quickly discovered the doctors had no medical answers to that question. The plain fact is, an answer would have done nothing to solve the problem. It would merely have given a plausible reason for the problem.

Of lingering concern were other questions that were fueled by anger, pity, guilt, and fear:

- *Why would God send us a baby with so many problems?*

- *What did we do to deserve this problem?*

- *What will life be like for this child as he grows to adulthood?*

- *Will he be accepted by his peers, or will he be a subject of ridicule and rejection all his life?*

Although these may be questions that all parents ask about their children at some point in response to some circumstance, these questions seemed of even greater importance to my parents as they dealt with the challenge of raising a child with a disability.

Through the years, I have faced my own questions. Both those I have asked myself and those others have asked me. People quite frequently ask, "John, do you believe God created you without arms for a reason?"

My response usually has two parts. I say, "You can say (*a*) God created me without arms to fulfill a mission, or (*b*) God gave me a strong will and put me among loving people to help me deal with not having arms. Either way, God has been working in my life from its beginning, and that knowledge alone is good enough for me."

I prefer not to speculate about how God thinks. No person can fully comprehend God's methods or ways. The Bible makes that very clear when it declares that God's ways are higher than our ways. We simply cannot understand the reason for many things that occur in our lives, in part because we cannot fathom the full scope of eternity, which is the true context of all that happens.

When a person asks me about God's intentions for my life, I suspect that he is really searching for an answer to the age-old question, "If God is a loving God, why does He make us suffer?"

I learned a long time ago that asking "why?" is futile. As a bitter and angry child, I often demanded that God give me an answer to my question, "Why didn't You give me arms?" I never received an answer to that question. Certainly nothing about my physical condition changed.

The end product of too many *why* questions is doubt, and doubt is one of the worst mental and emotional handicaps any person can experience. Doubt creates too many possibilities and too much ambiguity. Doubt doesn't give you anything to hold on to during tough times. Doubt doesn't give you anything to look forward to in the days ahead.

Eventually I learned that it is far more important, and far more effectual, to ask *what* questions:

- What do I have control over?
- What can I change?
- In what direction do I need to move today?
- What are my options?
- What are the possibilities?
- What are my resources?

Once I began to ask these and other *what* questions, I discovered all sorts of possibilities, and my circumstances began to change. I encourage others to redirect the time and energy they are expending in asking *why* questions to asking *what* questions.

WHAT SHOULD I ALLOW TO FLOW ON BY?

I recently was traveling on a day not at all suited for good travel. The flight was late in landing because a major storm had passed through the area, and planes were stacked up waiting to land. The airport was crowded with passengers, about half of them late arrivals hurrying to get out of the airport, and half of them passengers casually milling about or pacing in frustration as they waited to board a plane. Those who were hurrying tended to collide with those who were just casually walking about.

After considerable effort, I managed to get my luggage out

of the airport to the designated area where hotel shuttle buses came to pick up passengers. A man was already standing in the shuttle waiting area when I arrived there. He was a case study in impatience.

I could understand some of his frustration since a light mist was falling and the air was not only damp, but cold. Even so, we were under a canopy as we waited, and we really had little recourse. The airport pickup area was obviously congested, perhaps overly so because of the inclement weather. This man, however, became increasingly frustrated and angry the longer he waited for his shuttle bus to arrive. He occupied himself by voicing his displeasure at the long wait to anyone within earshot, and when he ran out of people to whom he could complain, he began to make one cellular phone call after another.

Finally the shuttle arrived. As it turned out, his shuttle was also my shuttle.

He boarded the bus and tossed his luggage onto the racks provided for passengers. I asked for and received help from the driver in getting my bags on board. At that point the man really saw me and realized for the first time that I have no arms. He seemed stunned by that realization. He slumped back in his seat, exhaled deeply and, after a moment's pause, said, "Here I am stumbling over a curb when you're climbing a mountain."

In my opinion, he said far more than he probably meant to say. Most people I know are stumbling over curbs—little obstacles they allow to frustrate, anger, or wound them emotionally. It might be an idle comment, a small delay, a traffic jam, a missing button, a small error in judgment, a slightly overheated remark from a total stranger, a miscalculation in timing. There's a great deal of life that we just need to allow to flow right on by us. We need to refuse to allow certain things to lodge in our minds or our hearts.

Certainly I am not advocating that a person live in denial or that a person swallow repeated hurtful remarks, only to allow that pain to fester until it reaches an explosion point. Not at all! Rather, I'm saying that unless a person is the recipient of a pattern of bad behavior exhibited by another individual or group, that person needs to let go of small annoyances.

I have found it helpful to spend a few minutes each morning in quiet reflection about my day ahead. I usually light a candle and sit in the upstairs alcove that is outside my bedroom and spend some time reading inspirational materials, praying, and just "being." I think through some of the events planned for the day and settle myself inside. There's no magic formula involved. Instead, this discipline gives me an inner pool of strength and calm from which to draw during the day.

Most people I know who are prone to quick anger or frustration get up in the morning and go at the day full steam ahead without any pause whatsoever to reflect on who they are and what they are hoping to both become and accomplish in life. They react to the moment rather than respond to life with a deep, inner sense of purpose and resolve.

If I allow someone else to give me a bad day, I am the one making the choice to receive that unwanted present. Unpleasant stuff happens; it just does. That's the harsh reality of life.

There are sufficient problems in any given day—from a late flight to a flat tire, from a rude waitress to a cup of bitter coffee, from a newspaper that got caught in a morning rain shower to a fellow driver who is overly eager to move when the lights change. If I allow the problems du jour to become problems du John—the problems of the day to become my personal problems—then I am the one who has taken on problems that aren't mine. I choose instead to let such problems remain in the world at large and to become an artful observer of them, not an active participant in internalizing them emotionally.

Can I avoid problems by refusing to internalize them? No. Am I living in a state of denial? No.

I try to learn from life's oddities and disruptive moments. The main lessons become ones involving character. It is in life's idiosyncrasies that we find the most important lessons about patience, tolerance, mercy, self-control, joy, inner peace, humility, and faith.

Life's peculiar situations give me time to explore my emotions and responses to life. How do I handle a situation? Why do I react the way I do? Am I handling a situation as well as I should handle it? Am I overreacting or underreacting? Why? It is in life's idiosyncrasies that we can truly learn about ourselves.

Would I prefer to go through each day without problems? Absolutely.

Am I willing to live in a constant state of frustration? Never!

I may not be able to solve all problems. But neither do I need to let problems rule me. I can choose how I will respond to them.

Some things can be fixed or altered. Some things can be endured. Some things can be valuable lessons. And some things simply *are*. It's a challenge for all of us to learn how to respond to irritants.

WHAT DO I NEED TO
RELEASE OR FORGIVE?

Bitterness and old feelings of hurt, anger, and rejection are weighty shackles on the soul. We are free to move forward only when we generally forgive those who have hurt us.

Forgiveness doesn't mean that a situation or deed didn't hurt.

Forgiveness doesn't mean that the situation wasn't significant.

Forgiveness doesn't mean that a person should not be held accountable for his actions or, in some cases, receive due justice for his actions.

Forgiveness means that I choose to let go of that person, that memory, that event, that deed, and move forward in my life. I choose to release the pain and go on.

Forgiveness isn't the same as forgetting.

I haven't forgotten that I was initially refused entrance to the Screaming Eagle Roller Coaster because I didn't have hands. But I forgave the person who tried to stop me from entering the ride. (After all, my brother Joe and I pointed out, most people raised their arms during the ride. They didn't use their arms and hands to hold on. That was an argument that couldn't be refuted, and I eventually went on the ride.)

I haven't forgotten that a teacher once gave me a D in handwriting. But I've certainly forgiven her. (After all, I score a lot higher in footwriting than most people!)

We never really forget any of the hurts or pangs of embarrassment we feel, but we have the capacity to forgive those who wittingly or unwittingly hurt us. In forgiving others, we are freeing ourselves.

Legend holds that Michelangelo was able to see a figure encased in a raw block of marble. He is quoted as saying that he chipped away at a block of marble to remove any piece that didn't look like the figure he had firmly in his mind, thus freeing the figure from its stone casing.

In many ways, our lives are sculpted by the mental and emotional handicaps we chip away from our souls.

WHAT IS THE MORE CREATIVE APPROACH?

A basic question more of us need to ask ourselves is this: *What is the most creative approach I can take to accomplish this task?*

To fully recognize all of our options, we often need to think outside the box. We need to turn on our God-given creative abilities and start to look for possibilities.

The famous impressionist master Claude Monet is reported to have said that he wished he had been born blind and subsequently gained sight so that he could have begun to paint without knowing what the objects before him were. His desire was to turn the rays of colored light that struck his retina directly into marks of paint on a canvas. He felt that having attitudes toward the objects he saw—in other words, knowing more about objects than what the eye saw—hampered this process.

Many of us are hampered by old ways of looking at things. We come to many situations and experiences with preconceived attitudes and time-worn habits. We need to begin to see with new vision.

Creative thinking may be as simple as looking at a condition from a different perspective—seeing something from another angle or another person's viewpoint.

Unfortunately most people I have met don't consider themselves creative. They believe that artists, musicians, and actors are the only people who are creative. I have studied art and enjoy painting, so I am always amazed at people who dismiss their creativity with statements such as "I couldn't draw a straight line if I had to" or "I have no sense of color at all." Creativity is not synonymous with artistic talent or the development of artistic skills. For that matter, most artists detest the ideas of straight lines and typical color combinations. Staying within convention implies conformity, and few things appall a true artist more than conformity.

The fact is, every person is creative. We all exercise our creative decision-making power every day in choosing what we will wear, how we will cut or style our hair, what types of houses we will live in and how we will decorate it, what types of cars we will drive, where we will choose to go, and what we will choose to do. Each person utters thousands of creative, never-before-uttered, uniquely put-together phrases in the course of any given month.

Developing your creative ability to see new options and new possibilities is essential to your ability to set goals and maintain the motivation necessary for reaching them. Creative insight is closely linked to vision. Without an ability to think new thoughts, we rarely see what can be. We are locked instead into what is. Helen Keller once said, "The greatest tragedy in life is people who have sight but no vision." I have a little adaptation on that: the greatest tragedy in life is people who have an asset and choose not to use it to full advantage.

To tackle the barriers I face every day, I must stay focused on what I *can* do and what might be possible. I must look at situations in a little different way to find solutions that work for me. Although I may feel somewhat anxious about trying something new or taking a physical risk, I cannot afford to close my mind to any possibility that holds out greater access to the world or ease in accomplishing a task. My condition forces me to find a way to pump gas into my car or change a lightbulb without arms, hands, or fingers. It's only by keeping an open mind, continually searching for new ways of solving problems, that I am able to see the solutions that sometimes exist in very unusual places.

WHAT IS THE RISK I NEED TO TAKE?

Perhaps the most potent *what* question you can and should ask yourself is this: *What is the risk I need to take to get beyond where I currently am to the place I want to be?*

Risks are always involved in growth. Identifying the risk—its exact nature and degree—is a vital step you must take if you truly are to maximize your potential.

I spent my elementary-school and junior-high-school years primarily in overcoming the physical challenges imposed by my unique physical condition. Once I hit high school, the mental and emotional challenges came to the forefront of my life.

Many of the challenges were those experienced by all teenagers, such as concerns about dating, fitting in, peer acceptance, my physical appearance, asserting independence from parents. I just had the added complication of having no arms.

When a girl I wanted to date told me, "Let's just be friends," I automatically assumed my condition was the reason. When my peers forgot to invite me along, I told myself, *It's because of my condition.* When my friends Neil, Doug, and Brian became heavily involved in basketball and cross-country, I felt abandoned. In retrospect, those were typical feelings that any teen would have felt. When you have an unusual physical condition, however, those feelings seem linked to your condition.

The one extracurricular activity that seemed to provide a level playing field for me was the church youth group. I engaged in church-sponsored service days, camp-outs, dances, sports tournaments, and special worship services. Whether visiting the residents of a local nursing home or attending a Cardinals baseball game in St. Louis, I felt like an equal among my friends. My condition rarely prevented me from full participation.

The most anticipated annual event on the youth-group calendar was the diocesan, or regional, youth convention. Young people from all over southern Illinois gathered at a major convention site to attend leadership and faith-building workshops. They also elected representatives and officers for the Executive Youth Council. Each candidate for a council position was required to present a short speech before all who had traveled to the convention and to run a minicampaign to promote him or herself.

For many teens in my area, pursuing an elected position was their first exposure to a political process. Those with the greatest willingness to talk and to expend energy were given an opportunity to shine. On the actual election day, the atrium of the convention facility was electrified as the teens who had decided to run for office nervously and eagerly solicited the support of their peers.

For the vast majority of us who attended the conventions, running for office was the farthest thing from our minds. The very idea of drawing attention to ourselves by campaigning and giving a speech was unthinkable. Especially those who were more reserved tended to look at the kids who campaigned for office as hotshots or weird. During some conventions, the adult leaders had difficulty in persuading enough young people to run for office. The chances for failure and a subsequent loss of respect were just too high.

Believe me, at that stage in my life, the last thing I wanted was for my friends to think of me as a geek. I couldn't imagine ever putting myself into a position of being more embarrassed or more rejected than I already felt. Simple participation in my local youth group satisfied me.

Mr. Darr, my junior-year religion teacher, had other ideas.

One March afternoon as I scurried to gather my notebook and papers off the floor—where I routinely laid them in order to take notes by writing with my feet—Mr. Darr approached me. A gentle and insightful man, he sat down in a desk across the row from me and asked, "John, are you going to the youth convention next month?"

"I'm planning on it," I said.

"You know there's only one person running for president at this time, and no one is running for treasurer," Mr. Darr said in a soft, matter-of-fact voice.

"Yeah," I said nonchalantly, wondering why he was telling me this.

"Well, John," he continued, "I've been thinking. You've really been involved in the youth group since your freshman year. A lot of people in the area know you. Have you ever thought about running for an office?"

I was stunned. "Me?" I replied with astonishment. "Why me?"

Mr. Darr took no notice of my raised eyebrows. "This year will be a busy one. I think it will also be a very exciting one for the new leaders. We have the diocesan centennial celebration coming up, the national youth conference in Pittsburgh, and the pope is visiting Los Angeles. If you were elected, you'd go to some of these events. I think this could be an excellent opportunity for you to grow as a leader."

I couldn't believe Mr. Darr was having this conversation with me. The more he spoke, however, the more I felt excitement starting to well up inside me. The idea that he thought I could represent my peers at such important events was flattering to me.

Mr. Darr gave me more details about the various events that council leaders would attend, and I started to conjure images of prestige. *People will respect me. I'll make new friends. I won't be overlooked. I'll be doing something better than participating in those stupid sports programs that I can't take part in.* Suddenly I caught myself daydreaming and yanked myself back into the conversation. "There's no way. I can't do it," I said. "What if I lose?"

Mr. Darr would not be deterred. "Well, that's the risk you take. But, John, I know you can handle it. I think you'd have a good shot at winning." His confidence in me made me feel good.

As much as the thought of running for office scared me, I also was intrigued by the challenge. I wanted to do something meaningful with my life—and this seemed meaningful.

"OK, I'll do it," I finally said. "But what position should I run for?"

A big grin spread across Mr. Darr's face, and he said, "Well, if you are going to run, you may as well go for the top."

In the next three weeks, I hurriedly put together a campaign to run for president of the regional youth organization. My opponent was a young man who had already been elected to the Executive Youth Council the previous year. He had experience on his side, plus he was well-known and liked among the youth.

Although I had attended conventions for two previous years, I felt like an outsider. I intuitively knew that if I wanted to win, my campaign had to be well organized and well executed.

I used my footprint as a campaign symbol and had it stamped on posters that a couple of my friends helped me make in art class. I asked Mr. Manwaring, my public speaking teacher, to help me write my campaign speech. We carefully calculated and crafted every word of my speech; I referred to my footprint and linked it to my desire to follow in the footsteps of Christ and take whatever steps were necessary to be a success in His eyes. I knew my talk was going to be different from any speech the young people had heard before, and the more I worked on my speech, the more excited I became to deliver it.

Finally the convention arrived, and more specifically election day arrived. When the time came for me to speak, a hush fell over the audience. As I walked to the podium, my heart was beating hard, and I had to struggle to fight down feelings of stage fright. The air was static with intensity. Everyone's eyes were fixed on me. I couldn't believe all those kids were giving me their attention, yet I could hardly wait to tell them what I had come to say.

Like a garden hose that spurts before flowing smoothly, my first words were sputtering ones. Very quickly, however, words began to stream gracefully from my lips. When I looked up from my notes to gain eye contact with those in the first few rows, I sensed that my words and stage presence were captivating them. The kids seemed to be sitting on the edges of their seats, soaking up every word I said.

I had no idea that my campaign speech would be the first of thousands of speeches I would give in my life. All I knew was that I was enjoying what I was doing, I was feeling effective and influential, and I was saying something that I truly believed was important.

After a very brief pause at the conclusion of my speech, the crowd stood and applauded enthusiastically. The sound roared through the corridors, and later that afternoon, I was elected president of the youth organization.

Throughout the remainder of that day, teens and adults offered me their congratulations with hugs and pats on my back. The victory was not mine alone, of course. My friends who were there shared in the triumph. It was a high moment for my local church and for my school. It was the first time in more than ten years that a student from our high school had been elected to a regional office. The school newspaper featured an article about my campaign, and my friends bragged about my success to kids they met from other schools. Mom and Dad were proud that I had taken a risk and succeeded.

Two days after my election, I was still on an emotional high when I received a phone call from the diocesan youth director, Colette Kennett. She had an official job for me to do. She had been contacted several weeks earlier by Mr. Daiber, a man who worked with the Adopt a Parish missionary organization. Mr. Daiber was seeking youth leaders to help carry out service projects and fund-raisers to benefit the poor people in Haiti. He asked Colette to choose two youth representatives to travel to Haiti to select a hospital, school, or orphanage for our regional youth to sponsor. Along with medicines donated by area hospitals, we had a $1,200 check to deliver to the Haitian Les Cayes Parish. Since I was the newly elected president, Colette asked me if I would represent the youth of southern Illinois in Haiti. I proudly accepted the challenge.

I was eager to go to Haiti to help the people there.

Instead, a poor child in Haiti ended up helping me.

For many people, the time has come to get off of their pity pots.

Eleven

ARE YOU SPIRALING DOWNWARD OR UPWARD?

THE TEMPERATURE HAD ALREADY CLIMBED WELL INTO the eighties by 8:30 the morning I arrived at Mother Teresa's Hospital for Children in Port-au-Prince, Haiti. The hospital was nothing like any hospital I had ever been in. Located at the end of a quiet and narrow street, it was a single-story, two-room concrete bunker with a rusty tin roof.

Before entering the hospital, I tried to convince myself that what I was about to see might be appalling, but I would handle it maturely. Once the car door was opened and I stepped out into the street in front of the hospital, I realized I was wrong. No one could have prepared me for the sights and smells that assaulted my senses.

A warm breeze dragged the stench of an open sewer through the heavy humidity of the morning. I quickened my pace to get into the hospital to escape both the heat and the stench.

Once inside the hospital, I almost tripped over a sick child who was asleep on the bare concrete floor. He was wrapped only in a dirty, tattered blanket. I was surprised that the nurses would allow such a thing. The surprises were to continue.

I had been in the hospital only a few moments when I detected the penetrating odor of urine. I heard coughing and wailing cries from tiny hoarse voices in the next room. With rising apprehension I turned to my right and entered that room. I immediately understood why that young child was sleeping on the floor by the front door.

The room was filled with old white cast-iron baby beds similar to those I had seen in movies depicting life in orphanages and hospitals in the 1930s and 1940s. There must have been at least twenty beds crowded into that one room, and each was occupied by a tiny malnourished bit of human life. The children ranged in age from a few months old to about ten years old. Most were skin and bones, their bodies in such a fragile state that every bone was visible and countable. Each child looked to me as if someone had taken an artificial skeleton from a high school biology lab and wrapped it in brown plastic.

In spite of their dark skin, most of the children had distended stomachs with protruding navels—all of which are classic symptoms of malnutrition. Their eyes were glassy and expressionless. A few of the children were crying loudly. None of them turned their heads or even blinked their eyes to acknowledge that a stranger had entered the room. I couldn't tell if they were delirious or just didn't care. I was afraid the reason might be they were close to death.

I couldn't help wondering, *Do they even know we are in the room? Have they ever known what it was like to be healthy and to have energy and to run and play? Are they scared? Are they lonely?*

As I stood there feeling overwhelmed by all that I was seeing, smelling, hearing, and thinking, I watched a nurse administer an intravenous shot into the scalp of an infant who didn't have enough muscle tissue on his limbs to support the needle.

Pity and terror boiled in me. Suddenly I had a flashback to my experience when I was confined to a hospital at the age of two. It is the earliest memory I have.

At the time, I was being fitted and tested for artificial arms at the Shriners Hospital in St. Louis. In those years, most physicians held to the opinion that a child should be fitted for a prosthetic device as soon as possible. The thinking was that the earlier a child wore such a device, the more readily the child would adjust to it.

I couldn't understand why I had been left at the hospital. It was a scary place to me. The doctor who came to my bedside was usually accompanied by a group of medical students. I certainly didn't know at the time that they were medical students. All I saw was a group of people in white coats, using long words I didn't understand, all the while prodding and poking my shoulders. I felt comfortable only for the few minutes each day when Mom and Dad were there. They drove a little more than an hour one way to get from our home to the hospital. Sometimes they brought along my three older brothers, and the four of us boys would play with the toys in the family lounge.

When the time came for my family to leave, terror gripped me. I remember kicking and screaming as the nurses held me, and Mom and Dad walked out the door. I feel certain the experience was awful for them, too, but they had no choice but to leave me there by myself. In those days, the hospitals did not permit parents to spend the night.

My bed was located next to the window that overlooked the visitors' parking lot. Even with tears flooding my eyes, I could see my parents and brothers get into the family station wagon and drive away. I remember crying out for them, sobbing and gasping for breath in between cries. They never heard my cries, of course. And the minute the car pulled out of the parking lot and drove out of sight, I was left to my own fears and feelings of being trapped and abandoned.

I had been, at least in some way, where these children in Haiti presently were. Great sadness and compassion for them filled my heart.

Just then, I was pulled from my reverie by something grabbing my waist. I looked down to see a little boy with his arms locked around me. He appeared to be about five or six years old, although the nurses later told me he was closer to ten. His big brown eyes peered up at me, and he had a faint smile on his face.

He didn't say a word. He didn't need to. The look in his eyes told me that he wanted me to pick him up and hold him. He wanted from me the one thing I couldn't give to him.

The thought rang through my mind like a bell clanging louder and louder: *You don't have the hands to pick him up. You don't have the hands to pick him up! YOU DON'T HAVE THE HANDS TO PICK HIM UP!* I couldn't think of anything else. I stood looking intently at him, desperately wanting to grab him and hold him tight. He continued to hold my waist and stare into my eyes. I couldn't maintain eye contact with him. I felt as if he were gazing into my soul, and I felt tremendously inadequate. Still, I didn't have the strength to turn away.

Tears filled my eyes. The last thing I wanted was for the boy to see me cry. I knew he had experienced a great deal of pain in his young life, and he didn't need to see more tears from me. I was disappointed in myself—not only that I could not pick him up, but that I was adding to his pain with my tears. I could not understand why he sought me out.

Up to that point, I was usually on the receiving end of love. For the first time I could recall, someone was actively seeking my love and my support and my embrace. I was disgusted that I had nothing to give.

An avalanche of frustration broke loose in me. *Why didn't he go to one of the other adults in the room? Doesn't this kid understand why I can't pick him up? Why, oh, why, don't I have arms to hold him?*

The automobile ride back to the missionary house was silent. The others in the group had seen what had happened between the boy and me, but none of them knew what to say. That evening I sat out on the veranda alone, slowly rocking in the rocking chair, replaying the scene in my mind, and asking God to give me some explanation about why the boy had come to me and had clung to me as he had. *What are You doing? What are You trying to say to me?*

I spent an entire week visiting hospitals, schools, and orphanages in various parts of Haiti. All week I was walking among disease, starvation, and death. The sights of grown men with leprosy and AIDS, a mother begging for food to feed her hungry children, an entire family living on a bed of trash in an open sewer. The scenes I encountered were shocking and sickening. The most vivid image in my mind, however, was that of a little boy's face as he clung to my waist in the children's hospital.

I was more than ready to leave the poverty and sickness of Haiti, yet I wasn't ready to go home. I knew my family would be eager to see me and would want to see my photographs and hear my stories, but I wasn't ready to talk about my experiences there. I felt deep restlessness in my soul, and I couldn't escape it.

On the return flight from Port-au-Prince to Miami, I tried to leave behind the images of Haiti that continued to fill my mind, but I couldn't. The intense gaze of that little boy as he wrapped his arms around me was more than a bad dream. It was real. It was part of me. It was embedded in my heart.

The more I thought about that little boy, the more my thoughts turned to painful experiences in my past. I recalled the frustration I felt when I couldn't dress myself. I recalled the doubts I had about whether I would ever learn to drive a car. I mulled over situation after situation in which I had felt helpless, alone, or sad. The more I thought about that little boy, the sorrier I felt for myself: *You'll never get over this stupid handicap. Why do you even try to live a normal life? You can't even help a little kid.*

If you had been with me on that flight, you probably would have asked, "Who is the victim here? The Haitian boy who is suffering from malnutrition and faces a life of poverty, or John wallowing in his self-pity?" The answer was clearly, "John."

I had allowed a victim mentality to overtake me.

A VICTIM MENTALITY IS A DOWNWARD SPIRAL

When someone has a victim mentality, he is consumed with self, and his focus is on the most pathetic aspects of his past or present. While he thinks he has been mistreated by life, in actuality, he is flushing away his life in a downward spiral of wounded emotions, constant worry, distorted perceptions, and cynicism. The person who adopts a victim mentality has little ability to recognize his options and virtually no motivation to pull himself out of the downward spiral.

The person with a victim mentality feels that the whole world is beating up on him, causing him pain and suffering. He becomes totally consumed by negative thinking: *I'm no good. It'll never work. I can't do it. There's no use.* He doesn't consider that every person faces tough conditions and challenges in life.

The person with a victim mentality fails to recognize that even though someone may have victimized him in the past, he is responsible for how he acts in the present. Furthermore, he is the only person who has the power of choice to remain in or to reverse a victim state.

Those who nurse a victim mentality over time eventually make "victim" their identities.

Trying to help someone with a victim mentality is like playing a mental game of tennis. Every time you hit the ball of responsibility into his court by proposing a solution, the victim knocks it back with an excuse about why your idea won't work. If you have ever become exasperated with such banter and walked away feeling as if you had tried everything to help without any success at all, you probably were right!

As long as you offer solutions that a victim can smack down without even considering the solutions to be possibilities, you're doing all the work. The victim has no incentive to accept responsibility for helping himself. When you're involved in a mental tennis match that you can't win, you may be the one who needs to choose to quit playing the game. You probably need to say simply, "So what *are* you going to do about your condition?" You may need to kick him off his pity pot with tough love.

I was sliding into a victim mentality on that flight to Miami. I felt my encounter with the boy gave me the perfect excuse to lash out at God in a way that I hadn't in a long time. I belligerently said to Him in my heart, *I don't get it. I thought You wanted us to help one another. Aren't we supposed to give to others? I don't care if I can't play basketball with my friends. But You won't even give me arms to pick up and hold a small child. You're a cruel God!*

In my anger, I dared God to respond to me.

A moment later, the thought flashed into my mind. *That little boy didn't want me to pick him up and hold him. He was hugging me!*

I had been so engrossed with my personal limitations that I had failed to recognize the simplicity and magnitude of his gift to me. In one moment, that little boy did something I had struggled my entire life to do. He looked straight past my physical condition, totally accepted me, and responded to me with love.

Wow!

The little boy had given me the extravagant gift of unconditional love. And I almost failed to recognize it and receive it. Instead, I turned his small and beautiful gesture of love into a neurotic meltdown.

In an instant, all my conditions and insecurities were revealed for what they were: Trivial. The political corruption, violence, disease, starvation, and death that plagued the Haitian people were real physical problems. My challenges were nothing compared to their hardships. The poor Haitian people literally lived on the edge of life. My limitations were largely self-imposed.

My mind raced through the times when I had allowed pity and anger to consume me, only I saw those instances in an entirely new light. I recognized that in each incident I had spent more time wrestling with my attitude than I had spent in figuring out how I would physically meet each challenge. My attitude, not my lack of arms, limited me. My real disability was in my mind and heart, not in my body.

In my work as a counselor, I encounter a number of people who suffer from a victim mentality. I suspect all of us adopt that mind-set from time to time. It's easy to let pity and fear blind us from taking an objective look at the real roots of our problems. It's far simpler to whine, "If only I had more money. If only I had more help. If only others wouldn't pick on me."

It's easy to allow doubt, prejudice, and ignorance to deafen us from hearing and absorbing words of genuine encouragement. It's far easier to moan, "Nobody cares. Nobody understands. Nobody loves me."

It's easy to shut ourselves off from others and become absorbed in self-pity. In so doing, however, we only separate ourselves from answers and help.

Don't misunderstand me. Not all feelings of anger, pity, loneliness, and fear are negative or unwarranted. Such feelings can help us correct an injustice or live through a loss. They are a normal part of grieving a loss—not only the death of a loved one, but a loss that can come in the form of a divorce, a miscarriage, a disability, a job loss, or a child leaving home.

Feelings of anger, fear, guilt, shock, loneliness, and discouragement are always present when we have failed at something important to us or have lost something or someone valuable to us. We are mourning not only the loss of the person or position, but also the death of the hopes, dreams, and aspirations we had connected to that person, position, or event.

The problem arises when we allow these feelings to become overheated in our minds to the point that they keep us from moving forward.

GROWTH IS AN UPWARD SPIRAL

How do we get back on track and create an upward spiral of growth?

1. Focus on the Future

We need to recognize that the life that lies before us is not the same as the life that lies behind us. None of us can go back and relive yesterday. None of us can embrace what has been irretrievably lost. However, we can choose to learn from the past and hold the best memories of the past and move forward into a bigger, brighter, and more beautiful tomorrow. We can choose to open ourselves up to discovering what the future may hold for us.

2. Embrace the Grieving Process

We need to recognize that grief doesn't really have an end. We never truly get over the loss of a relationship we valued; we never truly forget or move on from a love that was deep. There are always going to be events and moments when we suddenly find ourselves remembering the past and feeling sad for what we have lost. That's normal! It's perfectly acceptable, even healthy, to cry or to feel angry, sad, or lonely at times when grief rises to the surface of our lives. The response to moments of intense grief should not be a denial of emotions, but an expression of emotions followed by a choice to say, "I'm grateful for what I had. I'm grateful for what still lies ahead."

Some people need to face the fact that they have not yet

grieved over a major loss in their lives. I once delivered a speech to a group of saleswomen in Indiana. During the question-and-answer session after my presentation, a woman stood up and said to me with tears streaming down her face, "More than twenty years ago I gave birth to a baby girl who had a condition similar to yours. She didn't have arms, and she had a lot of other medical problems. She died within two days. I always rationalized to myself that her death was the best thing because she didn't have to suffer and lead a painful life. Listening to you speak about overcoming pain and having hope, I now realize that my daughter could have had a full life. I never allowed myself to feel sad about her death, but now I'm going to go home and do some grieving."

This woman had carried the pain of her daughter's birth and death with her for years, but she had never acknowledged that pain or dealt with it fully. She had never allowed herself to feel deep sorrow or to cry over her loss. Grief is important for us to experience if we truly desire to experience genuine peace as we move forward in our lives.

3. Accept the Compassion of Others

We need to recognize that when we are grieving, we need the understanding and compassion of others. We must never shut off those who desire to reach over and give us a hug or whisper to us, "It's OK. I understand. I care." Rather, we need to accept their help and support, and be grateful for it.

When I realized that the little Haitian boy was hugging me, not necessarily seeking a hug from me, I understood that he was giving me an "It's OK; I understand; I care" message.

I accepted the compassion he gave me. In my heart I hugged him back.

4. Start Helping Others

We need to turn ourselves inside out. One of the most effective ways to get out of the downward spiral of self-pity is to start helping someone else.

Helen Keller, who spent most of her life without sight and hearing, wrote this in her autobiography *The Story of My Life*:

> Everything has its wonders, even darkness and silence, and I learn, whatever state I may be in, therein to be content. Sometimes, it is true, a sense of isolation enfolds me like a mist as I sit alone at life's gate. Beyond there is light, and music, and sweet companionship; but I may not enter. Fate—silent, pitiless—bars the way . . . So I try to make light in others' eyes my sun, the music in others' ears my symphony, the smile on others' lips my happiness.

Despite all that she couldn't sense or do, Keller found a way to participate fully in life by helping others. In my own way, I made a similar choice.

As I embraced the fact that the little Haitian boy had expressed compassion and unconditional love to me, I had a strong urge to go immediately from my arriving flight in Miami to the departures area and take a plane back to Haiti so I could tell him, "Thanks. I needed that hug. I care for you too!" I felt as if I had unfinished business.

I knew, however, that an immediate return to Haiti was impossible. So I turned my mind to the questions, *What might I do to lift up this boy and others like him? What might I do to show love and concern for him? What might I do to give this boy a hug with my heart, if not with my arms?*

Ideas flooded my mind as I boarded the plane for the flight to St. Louis.

I could use my new office of youth council president to make people back home aware of those who suffer in poverty.

I could write a speech, put together a slide show, and tell people about my encounter with this little boy.

I could lift up this boy in prayer.

I could encourage others to lift up him and others like him through their prayers and donations.

The more I thought about the possibilities, the more excited I became. Remember, I was a teenager at the time. My energy level was high, and my determination was strong!

I had no idea at the time that in setting out to lift up this little boy, I was laying a foundation for my speaking career. In helping him, I was setting the stage for helping myself. In raising up his need before others, I was establishing a message of hope that would find numerous expressions through the coming years to a wide range of audiences who were dealing with a wide range of concerns. I knew at the time only that I had been given something that was important and meaningful to do—I had a mission to accomplish.

During my term as president of the youth organization, I went with Colette, the youth director, nearly every week to speak to a youth group, church, or civic organization. Sometimes we spoke more than once a week. One speaking event always seemed to lead to another, and we never turned down an opportunity to tell about the Haitian people or the plight they faced as they lived out their days in poverty, hunger, and pain. By the end of my term, I had codelivered more than sixty presentations throughout southern Illinois and we had raised more than eight thousand dollars for the poor people of Haiti.

Our presentations captured the attention of several small-town newspapers that featured articles about our work. Once

I stepped into the public eye, schools and civic organizations such as Rotary and Jaycees took note not only of my message about Haiti, but also the daily motivational challenges I personally faced in learning to live without arms. I was invited to give speeches about how to develop self-esteem and overcome adversity. By the time I reached college, I had addressed several conventions and corporations. That work continued while I was in college. I found the lecture circuit so appealing that I made speech communication my college major.

While I was a junior in college, I was asked to speak at a Total Quality Management seminar sponsored by the United States Defense Department. The meeting was scheduled in Colorado Springs. The platform was to be graced by America's most sought-after motivational speaker, Zig Ziglar.

I was obviously excited at hearing that Zig Ziglar was going to be present at the event. It never dawned on me he would actually be in the audience as I spoke, but there he was, sitting in the front row and taking notes. He waited until after I had greeted all those who came forward to meet me after my talk, and that meeting between the two of us was the start of a warm friendship.

After I graduated from college, Zig invited me to join his organization. I became the first professional speaker the Ziglar Corporation hired from outside its own ranks. At age twenty-one, I moved to Dallas to work as a speaker and trainer. Zig personally trained me as a protégé, and I was eager to be one. He helped me hone my public speaking skills, and as a member of his professional team, I had many exciting opportunities to address all sorts of audiences, from pastors to prisoners, from florists to defense contractors.

I still work with the Ziglar Corporation, although not

directly for the corporation as an employee. I still am speaking a message that is rooted in a desire to lift up others.

What began in Haiti continues.

One hug from one boy in one encounter—it was a meaningful gift to me, a remarkable turning point in my life, a deep message to my heart.

You probably have no idea what impact your life can have on others. Are you willing today to reach out and love someone unconditionally? Are you willing to let someone know you care? Are you willing to give something to alleviate the hurt in someone else's heart?

In giving to others, you are opening up yourself to receive a tremendous reward. You are opening up yourself to receive love.

Somebody you know needs your blessing today.

Twelve

ARE YOU AWARE THAT YOU ARE BLESSED TO BE A BLESSING?

I MADE MY FIRST INTERNATIONAL TRIP WHEN I WAS six years old. The trip was an eighteen-day pilgrimage to major shrines and holy sites in Ireland and on the European continent, the highlight of which was an opportunity to see Pope Paul VI at the Vatican.

My father and I traveled together. We were part of a forty-one-member delegation sponsored by Victorious Missionaries, a branch of Our Lady of the Snows Shrine in Belleville, Illinois. The other people came from across the United States, with several from our area in Illinois. Most of the travelers used crutches or wheelchairs. My father was one of the able-bodied volunteers who went along to assist others in negotiating areas that were far from accessible to people with physical limitations. He and my mother decided I might also benefit from the trip. In particular, my parents were praying and trusting God that my hips would continue to grow and develop so that I would not need corrective surgery.

The year before the trip, physicians told my parents that although my hip sockets had grown to enable me to walk, I would need to undergo a hip operation by the time I was eleven or twelve. The operation would place steel pins into my hips, and I would be required to spend at least six months in a body cast—not a pleasant thought for either a young boy or his parents. Only one physician took a "let's wait and see" attitude toward that prognosis. He recommended that nothing be done surgically unless my condition began to deteriorate. My parents took hope in his position, and my father took me with him on the trip with that hope and a great deal of faith that I would experience a blessing from God and my hips would stay strong and grow even stronger. They couldn't know it yet, but my hip sockets would develop, and I never needed surgery on them.

The rest of the pilgrims were seeking both physical healing and spiritual renewal. At Lourdes in France and at the Shrine of Our Lady of Knock in Ireland, group members entered the traditional baths that have been associated with healing miracles through the centuries. The highlight of the trip was a papal audience at St. Peter's Basilica.

Dad and I were seated on the front row in the basilica. I remember looking around at the building, especially at the members of the Swiss Guard who were standing at either side of the room. They were so serious and immobile that I finally concluded they were statues and not human beings. Before long, I got a little bored and was using my toes to play with a rosary to occupy the time.

Pope Paul VI noticed me tying knots in a rosary and asked that I be brought to him. According to those who were paying more attention than I, he said, "Bring me the bambino without arms. I want to give a special blessing to this child without arms who can do much with his feet. He is very good. I think he needs the blessing, and I wish him a happy life."

I had no idea that was happening until the Swiss Guards began to move toward me. I was shocked that they could walk! Dad and I were escorted to the pope, Dad by that time in tears, and the pope gave me a blessing, kissed me, and handed my father a little leather pouch that held a special papal medal.

I believe two things happened in that brief encounter. First, Dad received an incredible blessing—he was overwhelmed and very grateful. In some ways, I believe that experience validated to my father that God was deeply concerned about my life and that He had a special purpose for me. My parents no longer saw my disability as tragic but as part of God's plan and purpose for me.

And second, I received a blessing, although it has taken me a number of years to put it into full perspective.

I was not healed in that moment. Perhaps I should say, I did not grow arms in that moment. My hips were not instantly straightened or fully strengthened in that moment. What did happen? I believe I received an impartation of spiritual strength to endure what could not be changed and to persevere in overcoming what could be overcome.

Isn't that what a blessing really does for any of us? It gives us the strength to accept and endure what is, and what cannot be changed. It gives us the fortitude to face with courage and a conquering spirit what can be changed.

When parents bless their children, they are saying to them, "I'm glad God made you just the way He made you. I believe in your purpose on this earth. I love you for who you are, not what you can and cannot do. I encourage you to submit your life to God's care and love, and to do what you can to make this world a better place."

DO YOU FEEL BLESSED?

Of one thing I am very certain: we are all called to experience, in some way and at some time and by some means and through some person, an affirmation regarding our creation and existence on this earth. If you have never received a blessing from someone, perhaps you will receive it from me.

In extending a blessing to you, I am not trying to put myself into the shoes of a clergyperson and certainly not a pope. I do not offer a blessing to you because I am trying to proclaim myself as being more spiritual or more spiritually mature than you. Rather, I offer a blessing to you as a fellow traveler on the journey of life. I affirm you as God's child. I bless you for being you—a one-of-a-kind creation of God. I bless you for being precisely who God designed you to be, fully equipped with unique talents and abilities, dreams and goals, and a personality that is capable of expressing joy and hope and love. I bless you as a child of God who has been given potential for growth and development. I bless you as a child of God who is empowered by God to

- learn more than you presently know,
- develop and express a more positive attitude than the one you presently have,
- engage in relationships that become even deeper and more meaningful than they are presently, and
- grow in faith more each day.

God has a special plan for your life, and I affirm that in you.

A GREATER AWARENESS OF THE WORLD

The Latin root for the word *education* means "to lead out." Knowledge truly leads us out of the darkness of ignorance and despair. Knowledge gives us greater control over our world and increases the options available to us.

I like what Eric Hoffer has said: "In times of change the learners shall inherit the earth, while the learned will find themselves beautifully equipped to deal with the world that no longer exists."

In referring to learning, I'm not talking about formal degrees. Even though I have two college degrees, I hold to the opinion expressed by Mark Twain: "I have never let my schooling interfere with my education." Education is the end product of learning, and we are all capable of learning more than we presently know.

Sound, accurate, useful information is nearly always a blessing to those who will receive it and apply it. So many limitations can be overcome by the acquisition of information. For example, those who have the condition of illiteracy are blessed when they learn to read.

The limitation you may be facing in your career, or in your family life, may be rooted in a lack of practical skills. You may need to learn to type, to use a computer, to manipulate an iron, or use a cooking utensil.

When I was in college, I met a number of students who turned their white T-shirts blue by washing them with a new pair of jeans. They needed instruction about how to wash clothes.

One student I'll call Fred admitted he had never done *any* laundry prior to going away to college. He had no idea where to begin. When Fred ran out of clean clothes, he asked his roommate to wash some things for him. The roommate was happy to help. He put the clothes in the washing machine and later transferred them to the dryer. Then he said to Fred, "I've got to get to class. If you want any clothes, they're in the dryer."

Fred went to retrieve his clothes but couldn't find them. Later that day when his roommate returned, Fred said, "I thought you said my clothes were in the dryer. I couldn't find them." The roommate said, "Of course they're in the dryer, right where I left them." The two went to the laundry room, and sure enough, the laundry was in the dryer. Fred had looked in the washing machine for his clothes. He didn't know enough about laundry to tell a washing machine from a dryer!

Later, Fred decided he knew enough to do his own laundry. He filled the washing machine with dirty clothes, added soap, turned on the machine, and watched the tub fill with water. The machine never started to agitate, however, so Fred began to swish the water around vigorously with his hands and arms. When his roommate saw him doing that, he asked, "What are you doing?" Fred replied, "This thing never kicked in. I think it's broken." The roommate grinned, shook his head, and replied, "You have to close the lid in order for the machine to start agitating."

Talk about a need for instruction! Some people need more basic information than others.

In my work as a counselor, I frequently encounter people who have never learned how to express their emotions or how to choose appropriate behaviors. They don't know what to do with their excess anger or frustration. They don't know where to begin to deal with guilt, shame, or feelings of isolation born of rejection. They would benefit from the information offered in an anger-management course or assertiveness training.

Are your limitations today rooted primarily in a lack of information? If so, isolate what you believe you need to learn. Start with the basics of what you don't know and what you need to know. Just because you don't know how to set up a computer doesn't mean that you need to take a course in computer science. Start at the minimal level of what you don't know, and as your need to know and your interest expand, pursue further instruction.

There are countless parents who don't know what to do about their children who display continual anger or rebellion, or who may be involved with peers the parents consider to be negative influences. There are countless spouses who don't know what to do about their spouses who are abusive or who are addicted to alcohol, drugs, or heavy-duty painkillers.

If you don't know what you don't know, ask someone! Ask your supervisor at work what he would advise you to learn so that you will be prepared for promotions and raises in the future. Ask your career or guidance counselor at school, or at the college you attend, to give you advice about what courses you should take to prepare for a career you find interesting. Ask your pastor or a counselor what you should learn to do about a family or personal matter.

Don't attempt to function at a low level of performance because you are too proud to admit that you don't know. Ask experts. Seek instruction. Find sources of information.

We are all capable of acquiring more skills, adding to our information bases, and applying more of what we know to make our lives more productive and efficient. We are all capable of improving the quality of our lives through greater exposure to the things that we might label beautiful and beneficial—art, music, an appreciation for the grandeur of nature, cultural experiences, and spiritual retreats.

We are all capable of learning from the experiences we have—those that we choose for ourselves and those that happen to us without our willful consent. I learned some things from selling apples grown in our orchard near Breese. I learned other things by hiking the Batu Caves just a few miles north of Kuala Lumpur. I learned still other things from traveling to Spain with my younger brothers.

I encourage you to recognize that there is much *more* that you can learn and will benefit from learning. I encourage you to ask questions, seek out mentors, and read more books and magazines. I think you'd be amazed at how much your worldview may be expanded by reading a newspaper twenty minutes a day, and I don't mean just the sports and comics sections.

I bless you as a child of God who is capable of learning more about the way this world operates in order to better operate in this world!

AN ABILITY TO CHANGE YOUR ATTITUDE

Attitudes are a rather nebulous combination of thoughts, actions, and feelings. Although we may not be able to measure attitudes directly, we know that our attitudes are changed by what we think, what we do, and how we feel. In my life, I have found that if I change my thoughts and actions, a change in feelings follows. It's easier to change thoughts and actions than feelings. Feelings are strong and elusive; they are difficult to master or even define. Start with actions. Move on to thoughts. Feelings will fall into line.

Specifically pay attention to your self-talk. Monitor what you say to yourself. When you're in a bad mood, take a step back, and ask yourself, *What am I saying to myself about myself?*

When I work with depressed clients, I always ask them what they are reading. To date, they consistently have responded that they were reading something "dark"—horror stories, gruesome murder mysteries, or biographical stories about heinous criminals. I ban them from reading such materials while they are in therapy, and I insist that they read inspirational materials. What is taken into the mind feeds the mind.

I encourage you to pay renewed attention to what you are feeding both your body and your mind. Are you eating a healthy diet, getting adequate sleep, and doing enough exercise? Are you reading materials or watching programs and movies that are positive, instructive, or morally uplifting?

Garbage in, garbage out. It's an old saying but true. Most of us probably need to redefine "garbage in." As a culture, we seem to consume a great deal of morally void garbage without questioning the value or the impact of what we are mentally and emotionally taking into our lives.

Pay attention to what you do and with whom you associate. You can't help being influenced by your friends, associates, coworkers, and family members. Choose to spend time with people who will build you up personally, affirm the values you hold, and help you approach life with courage and a balanced perspective.

Negative thoughts and self-defeating actions often tend to

feed off each other. Before you know it, you can get sucked into a downward spiral of despair and end up on a pity pot.

I bless you today as a person who is capable of *choosing* to engage in positive behaviors, think positive thoughts, and express positive feelings.

DEEPENING FRIENDSHIPS CAN BE FORGED

People often speak of forming relationships or building friendships. When a romance ends, we tend to call it a breakup. These terms, in my opinion, put relationships into the category of engineered or constructed things. I prefer to think of relationships as analogous to living organisms, such as plants. Relationships grow at their own pace and have a life of their own. No one person can make a *relationship* work. It takes two people to be mutually responsible and willing participants.

Relationships don't grow overnight. They require time to take root.

Relationships don't end in a breaking process as much as they die from neglect, inappropriate care, or destructive behaviors.

The good news is that you are capable of entering into relationships and doing what you can to nurture their growth. You can choose to spend time with friends and family members, to share experiences, to be vulnerable in expressing your opinions, ideas, and emotions, and to go the extra mile in caring for others with generosity and a positive attitude.

C. S. Lewis once said, "The next best thing to being wise oneself is to live in a circle of those who are." I agree!

I bless you as a person who is capable of developing deep and abiding friendships and relationships in which you receive from others and give to those who can benefit from your insights and experience.

AN EVER-GROWING FAITH AND HOPE

As I move forward in faith, I have discovered that my need for answers to many of my questions about God, other people, and myself becomes irrelevant. The questions are no longer important because faith gives me permission to say, "Even though I don't understand fully, I believe; I hope; I love." Faith anchors me in the present moment and helps me to control stress and worry.

Faith, for me, flows out of prayer and service to others. Prayer alone is not sufficient. Neither is continual activity in serving others. For me, the balance of prayer and service is important—the one nurtures my relationship with God, and the other establishes my relationship with others.

Faith is vital for having a relationship with God. It's difficult to really love anyone, including God, without knowing him. I choose not simply to know *about* God, but to seek to know Him by conversing with Him daily—telling Him how I am feeling, what I am thinking, and the needs I desire for Him to help me meet. Conversing, of course, includes listening quietly and reflectively.

Faith can't be intellectualized. It is not the product of analysis. Jesus challenged His followers to come to God as little children (Matt. 18:2–4). Jesus kept faith simple, and I believe we need to do likewise.

I bless you today as a person who has the capacity to believe. I bless you as a person who has the potential to grow in faith and in relationship with God.

WHOM ARE YOU BLESSING?

Those who are blessed have the challenge and responsibility of becoming a blessing to others. Ask yourself today:

- Whom am I blessing? Whom am I affirming, encouraging, building up?

- Whom am I helping in practical ways?

- Whom am I *serving* with my love, talents, and resources?

My neighbor across the street, Jeanne, is a blessing to me. She blesses me practically and frequently by bringing me food—delicious, home-cooked, lovingly prepared, generously portioned, and freely given casseroles and breads and other gifts of food. Somewhat ironically Jeanne often gives gifts of foods that she cannot eat. She has a serious heart condition and has had bypass surgery, so many of the foods she loves to cook and give away are not ones she can personally enjoy. Her pleasure is not in eating her own cooking, but in giving away foods she knows others enjoy.

I am not the only person she blesses. According to her husband, Norval, she has been blessing people in this way for decades, even in the early years of their marriage when the two of them could hardly afford to feed themselves. Today, this exceedingly generous woman blesses my neighbor who lives to the east of us as well as me. This neighbor, who is paralyzed, was injured in a swimming accident years ago and now lives alone since the death of his parents. Home-health-care assistants monitor his medications and help him with matters of clothing, hygiene, and general home care and meal preparation. But his really *good* meals come from Jeanne.

Did my generous neighbor ask to have two disabled people move into her neighborhood and her life? No. We arrived within shouting distance of Jeanne's kitchen, and she chose to bless us in the way she knew to bless us.

I have a hunch that's exactly what God has in mind for each one of us. He wants us to look around at the people who are within range. There are enough needy people to go around—some with physical needs, some with emotional or family-related difficulties, some with spiritual problems, some with financial troubles, some with other practical areas of lack. It's up to us to open our eyes and our hearts and ask, "What can I do?"

And then when we have opened ourselves to the needs that are within reach, we need to ask God to give us the courage to reach out and meet those needs. It's not enough to send money afar or wish and hope that *somebody* will take care of the needs that our neighbors and church friends are experiencing. We are probably the "somebodies" God has in mind to do the caring! It's through our hands, feet, smiles, words of encouragement, and practical acts of service—and yes, even through casseroles, salads, cakes, and pies—that God chooses to spread our abundance to fill gaps.

ENCOURAGER OR DISCOURAGER?

One day I was back home in Breese reflecting upon the way God had blessed my life with a message and a mission when I had a chance to visit with my friend Carson. Carson is a third-generation funeral director, and he now owns four funeral homes in southern Illinois. He said to me, "You know, John, your job as a motivational speaker and my job as a funeral director are a lot alike."

I quipped, "What are you saying, Carson? People are just dying to hear me?"

Carson chuckled and said, "No, John. People often ask me, 'What is the toughest part of your job?' It's not all the eerie aspects of death that most people think would be difficult. The toughest part of my job is comforting the living people in the front parlor of the funeral home. My job is to help the living move on with life. John, that's your job too."

Carson was right. As long as we are alive, we face painful conditions. Each one of us confronts the task of getting through tough times and moving on. Each of us also has the opportunity to help others get through tough times and to encourage them to move on in life. We can choose to be encouragers or discouragers.

Encouragers embrace us in our pain and then point us toward our future with hope of what could be, might be, and still will be. Discouragers may embrace us, but they do nothing to help us let go of the burdens of the past. Rather, they assist us in dwelling on what might have been or what should have been.

Are you an encourager or a discourager?

What are you to yourself? Do you continually tell yourself, *Life is going to be better. Things are going to look up. This present pain will eventually end, and life in the future has the potential for being better than anything in the past*? Or do you tell yourself, *The best is over. Things are downhill from here. Nothing I ever do will ever be as glorious as what I have done*?

Your present is framed by the way you encourage or discourage yourself. Your future is shaped by the degree to which you encourage yourself, encourage others, and allow others to be a source of encouragement to you.

*A*sk, and it will be given

to you; seek, and you will

find; knock, and it

will be opened to you.

– Matt. 7:7

Thirteen

MY PARENTS WALKED A FINE LINE THROUGHOUT MY growing-up years of wanting to preserve my dignity and independence, and humbly accepting assistance from organizations such as the Variety Club, which helps provide artificial limbs to disabled children. Mom and Dad were like most people thrust into their situation. They didn't *want* to need help, but they nonetheless needed help. They had no knowledge of or experience with caring for a child with special needs. At the same time, they did know what was right for their family and themselves. It's a line we all walk—when to ask for help and when to be independent.

I walk that line every day.

A particularly challenging routine task is grocery shopping. When I go to the store on my own, the first challenge is dealing with a grocery cart. I have to lean my upper body in a hunched-over position on the handle of the cart to guide it with my shoulders. Trust me—I know every cart in Breese that has unbalanced wheels. Getting an obstinate cart down a long and straight supermarket aisle requires

169

concentrated effort. Try not using *your* arms, hands, or fingers for that task!

The cart represents only part of the challenge, of course. Grabbing a large item, such as a melon, or reaching for items on high shelves is tricky. Ever tried to lift a frozen turkey out of a chest-style freezer without the use of your arms or hands?

Suffice it to say, I lack enthusiasm for grocery shopping. It has always represented a major undertaking.

One morning a couple of years ago, as I was trying to motivate myself into enjoying the daunting process, I maneuvered my cart in such a way that I saw something new. Off to the side of the cash registers, and just behind the automatic front door, I noticed a miniature shopping cart. It looked like a regular cart in every way, except smaller. I assumed that the store furnished such carts to pacify children while they were shopping with Mom or Dad. Seeing the cart sparked a jolt of enthusiasm in me. *Why hadn't I thought of this before?*

The miniature cart was just the right size for my six-year-old niece, Emily. I began to think: *Emily is in the first grade and gets out of school at three o'clock. I can wait!* With a grin on my face, I retreated from the store and went back to my car.

Emily loved the idea of helping Uncle John grocery shop, and our shopping outings have become a fun time that we now share routinely. I generally pick up Emily after school, and we head to the supermarket. She grabs the miniature cart and graciously follows behind me. As we wander through the store, Emmy's sense of responsibility and maturity toward accomplishing our mission always impress me. She refuses to be distracted by all of the tantalizing colors and images on many products aimed at children. Instead, she stays focused on the job before us. She has yet to wander away or pester me for a treat.

Emmy's assistance does not end with merely pushing a cart. Although she is only a child, she has a long reach. She is able to grab some items that rest on higher shelves, and she is especially helpful when it comes to dealing with breakable items such as a carton of eggs or a bottle of juice. Without her help, I would have to risk grabbing these items with my teeth or chin. Believe me, before I began to shop with Emmy, I made a mess of things on more than one occasion.

I have always been proud of my ability to fend for myself. Asking a six-year-old niece to lend me a hand was humbling. Once I was able to get my pride out of the way, however, I found that the best possible solution for this particular problem was to be found in asking for and receiving help from another person.

The truth is, I benefit greatly from Emmy's help. Grocery shopping goes more smoothly, quickly, and safely. It's no longer a chore I dread, but an outing I genuinely enjoy. An added benefit of sorts has emerged since Emmy learned to read. She now recommends that I buy products labeled "fat free"!

I hope you won't conclude, however, that this has been an entirely Emmy-giving and John-receiving arrangement. Emmy has benefited in various ways that are important to *her*. Shopping with me gives her feelings of importance and maturity. She is able to get away for a little while from her two younger brothers, who like to pester her. And as we prepare to check out of the grocery store on each visit, I allow her to pick out a treat she wants.

Through the years, our relationship as uncle and niece has developed into one that is increasingly significant to both of us. In fact, we're looking for even more things we can do together. Our latest project is to learn German together using a computer CD program I purchased.

THE PREREQUISITE FOR RECEIVING HELP

There is only one basic prerequisite for receiving help from others: acknowledge your limitations and your need for help.

Acknowledging your limitations is a very different thing from using your limitations as an excuse. As a boy, I used my condition as an excuse for why I couldn't do certain things, why I shouldn't do certain things, and why others should help me. I took a major step in my life when I no longer expected others to do for me what I could do for myself. It's a noteworthy step toward self-responsibility anytime a person moves from expecting others to wait on him to waiting on himself.

At the same time, we need to be realistic about our limitations and our areas of weakness. We all have things we cannot do.

A friend told me about a young married couple she knows. The husband had just admitted to his wife something she had not known before they married: he suffered from night blindness; he simply couldn't see well enough at night to drive on the freeway or in areas that were not brightly lit. The young wife, in turn, had a confession for her husband—she suffered from dyslexia as a child. She learned to compensate for the condition to the point that she graduated from college and enjoyed reading novels during the times when, in the course of her work as a flight attendant, she had layovers in airports far from home. She admitted, however, that she still had trouble sewing or hitting a baseball with a bat.

The two had a great laugh when they completed their confessions. He said, "I may ask you to drive after dark, but I won't ask you to read the road signs!" She replied, "I'll drive our son to ball practice, but you're going to have to play catch with him at home!"

Limitations aren't necessarily severe. At times, they function in our lives more as nuisances or hindrances. At other times, our limitations are such that we *need* to ask others to help us. At still other times, we need to recognize that our unique physical conditions keep us from participating fully in some activities, although not from all related activities.

I know that I could spend an entire day taking golf lessons from Tiger Woods, and I may learn some pointers about golf in the process, but I am not going to improve my golf game. Dare I say it—my handicap is not likely to change.

The same goes for my tennis game. I can mentally practice my backhand swing all day and not see any improvement whatsoever in my baseline game.

I also know that if you and I are stranded on a desert island and you suddenly choke on a bit of coconut and need someone to hug you in the Heimlich maneuver, you may be out of luck.

There are some things I cannot do. I recognize these limitations. I just don't let them stop me from participating in life or enjoying life to the fullest.

HELP CAN SOMETIMES BE PURCHASED

There are times when the best way to overcome a limitation is to hire a professional or a qualified helper to do the job.

I once decided to spend a sunny Saturday afternoon painting my mailbox. I generally paint using my toes, but that time, I decided it would be smarter to hold the paintbrush in my teeth. And I decided to hold the container of paint between my chin and shoulder. Yes, it was awkward. And after I accidentally jabbed the pointed end of the paintbrush handle into the roof of my mouth, I decided that too much independence can be a dangerous thing! I hired a qualified painter to do the job.

I can operate a lawn mower, but why? Boys in the neighborhood are delighted to mow my lawn for a little extra spending money.

I can run a vacuum cleaner and scrub out a bathtub, but I'd rather pay someone to clean my house.

I can drive a car, but when I am speaking in major cities, I find it safer and more convenient to take a taxi or rely on shuttles or services provided by the organization to which I am speaking.

I can iron my shirts and pump gas at a gas station, but I prefer not to. I'd rather pay for full service at the gas station and let the dry cleaner do my shirts.

ASK FOR THE HELP YOU NEED

Not long ago I was buying a sandwich at a snack counter. I generally keep my driver's license, credit cards, and dollar bills in a small plastic folder that I put in my left shoe under the arch of my foot. When I need money, I slip off my shoe, lay the wallet on the floor, and pull the required bills out of the wallet with my toes. This time, however, a couple of bills stuck together, and before I knew it, my credit cards and driver's license had fallen out of the wallet. I had a variety of items scattered on the floor around my feet.

Of course, I was frustrated. I knew people behind me were waiting and watching. From the corner of my eye, I saw one person lunge to help me gather the items, but then he caught himself in midstoop. I knew he was confused about what to do. I felt sorry for him, even as I knew he was feeling sorry for me.

I turned and said, "I'd sure appreciate your help." He eagerly gathered up the items on the floor and put them in the wallet, which I then tucked back into my shoe. I thanked him, and we went on with our days. I refused to carry embarrassment from the store. I feel certain he carried from the store a certain amount of goodwill toward me and a feeling that he had done something nice for another human being.

Moments like these occur commonly between those who are so-called able-bodied and those with special needs. Many able-bodied people seem confused about whether to offer help. I am frequently asked, "When I see a disabled person struggling to do a routine task, such as open a door, should I jump in and help?"

My answer is this: "Ask the person, 'May I help you?'"

If the person says yes, then go ahead and assist. You have extended a common courtesy—something we all should extend more often. A mother carrying a child and juggling an armload of packages, or an elderly man with a cane, could also benefit from your assistance just as much as a person with a physical condition.

If the person says no, don't take his or her refusal personally. That person is trying to discover his level of independence. Be patient if you are forced to wait as the person struggles a little.

Don't automatically assume that the help you want to give is truly helpful. I've learned this lesson firsthand as I have traveled around the world.

Other societies tend to think that all handicapped people use wheelchairs and don't have use of their legs. I once landed at an airport in the Philippines and was greeted by an attendant with a wheelchair. He had been told that a handicapped person was aboard, and he automatically assumed I couldn't walk.

Let me assure you, that mind-set is prevalent. I often cringe when I am unknowingly assigned a handicap-accessible room at a hotel. The clerk at the front desk no doubt thinks he is doing me a favor, but in actuality, he's creating a much bigger problem for me. The counters and desktops are all higher in handicap-accessible rooms, and the bars placed on the sides of bathtubs are only one more obstacle I have to crawl over while maintaining my balance.

A question to ask a person with a unique physical challenge is this: "Would my doing this be helpful to you?" The very help you think would be welcome may be an added hindrance to a person.

All of us value independence because it gives us feelings of personal freedom. Independence in mobility gives us the freedom to go where we want to go. Independence in thought gives us the freedom to explore new ideas and to free ourselves of stereotypes and prejudices.

What we must come to value is not *dependence* upon others but *interdependence*. You help me; I help you. Your weakness can be an opportunity for me to display strength; my limitation can be your opportunity to use an asset.

Owning my home and living by myself give me a tremendous feeling of independence. But if the garage door or furnace breaks, I have a renewed sense of my dependency. When I can pick up a newspaper for a vacationing neighbor, and that neighbor in turn watches my house when I am away, I have an awareness of my interdependency. All three—dependence, independence, and interdependence—are appropriate in different situations and relationships.

Deciding what approach to take at which time and under what conditions is a trial-and-error method. Be willing to take the risks associated with trying. If you err, change your approach. Ask questions of others: "Am I overstepping my bounds?" "Is this a help or hindrance to you?" "What would you like for me to do?"

Be willing to ask yourself: *Am I helping in the short term but hurting in the long term? Am I developing a relationship that is basically a one-way street along which I always give and another person always receives? Am I using people for my own pleasure or gain? Am I manipulating others into serving me?*

The limitations imposed by my condition remind me frequently that success is relational. While most of us would like to believe that our single-minded determination, hard work, and brilliant ideas have made us successful, at some point, we must realize that such a conclusion is not only an error, but also a display of pride. All of us become who we are and achieve what we achieve in the context of other humans. It is by balancing our giving and our receiving in a healthy flow of ideas, energy, skills, and physical assistance that we achieve a win-win situation with those who live in close relationship to us.

GIVING AND RECEIVING HELP WITH DIGNITY

People have said to me on more than one occasion, "I admire your willingness to ask others for help. I usually feel too embarrassed or too humiliated to ask." I suspect part of their reluctance may be rooted in a belief that asking for help is a sign of personal weakness. Nothing could be farther from the truth. Asking for help is not a sign of weakness—it's a sign of shared humanity.

Many times, boldly asking for help sends a signal that you are confident in yourself as a human being, and that you are wise enough to recognize that no one person can do everything—but that we all can do something. In working interdependently, we can usually find a way to tackle almost any condition, circumstance, or problem and bring about a solution or at least an alleviation of negative symptoms.

I suspect another part of a person's reluctance to ask for help lies in a fear of personal rejection.

The fact is, a "no" does not necessarily mean rejection. There can be any number of reasons for a person to say no, including scheduling problems, a bad mood, fear, or a stress overload. If you get a "no" from someone, accept it at face value. Refuse to internalize feelings of rejection. And then ask another person.

As you might expect, I have difficulty dealing with the overhead bins on airplanes. I travel frequently in the course of my work as a motivational speaker, and I usually have carry-on luggage that I carry with the aid of shoulder straps. I can usually negotiate my way down an airplane aisle, but once at my seat, I cannot manage to hoist my bags over my head into the storage bins.

I usually ask a flight attendant to help me, and occasionally a fellow passenger will recognize my physical condition and offer assistance even before a flight attendant comes my way.

On one trip, I asked a flight attendant if she could help me put my bag in the overhead storage area, and she promptly replied, "No, I can't. It's against airline policy for me to lift bags for passengers."

"It is?" I asked politely. It was the first time I had ever heard about such a policy.

"Yes," she said matter-of-factly. "Too many flight attendants have experienced back difficulties from helping passengers with heavy luggage." Then she added, "You have to be responsible for your own bag. If you can't get it in the overhead bin, you must put it under the seat in front of you or check it."

There wasn't much chance of that since I was sitting in the front row. Fortunately for me, the man seated across the aisle from me jumped in and said, "Here, I'll get it for you."

I'm not certain the flight attendant recognized as she was speaking to me that I have no arms. I was wearing a jacket, and she might not have noticed. For me, her lack of kind help was a rebuff, but it wasn't something I was going to allow to ruin my day or my flight.

As much as possible, I try to fly in the first row of the first-class section of an airplane. That gives me sufficient leg room to spread any papers or books on the floor in front of me to work, make notes, or sketch ideas. It also allows me room to have a meal tray put on the floor so I can eat using my toes to hold a fork or spoon.

When the flight attendant noticed me working with my feet and toes, she came to me, knelt by my seat, and apologized for her earlier statements. "I could have been more helpful," she said. "I'm sorry." I thanked her for telling me that. Her apology and my acceptance of it healed what distance had been created between us.

So often that is the case in all of our lives. A simple heart-felt apology and a sincere acceptance of it can help us get past things that might have been said in haste, frustration, or anger. It also created a bridge for the woman to help me in other ways as the flight progressed.

She had helped restore my dignity and, in a way, I had helped restore hers.

Far more important, however, than knowing that others are treating you with dignity is for *you* to maintain your sense of dignity. That occurs when you know that you have acted with kindness and integrity, generosity and empathy, and without prejudice or condescending pity. If you truly have been a good soul to someone else—through encouraging words, helpful actions, or a friendly smile—you can rest assured that you have done the right, decent, and good thing. If someone fails to acknowledge your goodness, or fails to appreciate it, you nevertheless can acknowledge your goodness and worth.

BE GRATEFUL FOR
THE HELP OTHERS OFFER

I am exceedingly grateful for the help offered to me just recently. I was riding the Metro Link, the rail transportation system from downtown St. Louis to the airport. I was sitting by the window and thinking about the speech I was sched-uled to deliver in Dallas the next morning. From seemingly out of nowhere, a man came and sat in the seat next to me. His clothes were dirty and he was unshaven and smelled of body odor. He started to pick up my suitcase.

Quickly putting my foot on the bag to stop him, I asked,

"What are you doing!" He let go of the bag and said, "Man, I know you are going to the airport and have money. I need some money. Can you give me a couple of bucks?" Startled and a bit annoyed, I said, "No, I don't have anything to give you."

I had been panhandled in Chicago and New York, and generally speaking, when I said no, the panhandlers moved on. This man, however, persisted. He grabbed my leather coat, pulling it open and ripping off a button in the process, and said angrily, "Man, I know you've got money. I just got out of prison." He reached into his dirty coat and pulled out some pink papers. Moving right into my face, he said, "These are my parole papers. I need some money."

The smell of liquor on his breath was strong and I noticed his front teeth were knocked out. By then I was scared. I wanted out of the situation. I flung my coat and empty shirt-sleeve from my left shoulder so he could see my condition as I said very directly, "I don't have any arms. Can you please let me go?" I was hoping to appeal to his sense of compassion, but he continued his demand, showing little more than momentary surprise. "I'm sorry, man, I'm sorry, but I need money. Just give me some money!"

I could tell he was looking me over frantically to see where I might keep my wallet. He began patting me down to try to find my wallet, and I realized he wasn't going to give up.

I turned to a businessman, dressed in a suit and tie, who was sitting directly behind me and who was watching the scene play out. I said to him, "Sir, I don't have any arms. I need some help here." He nodded, stood and moved into the aisle, and said, "Come back here and sit with me. Sit next to the window." He moved to shield me from the mugger, and I got up and began to move myself and my suitcase.

The mugger became angry, loudly accusing the business-man of "interfering" and telling him to "mind your own business." Then he began pushing and shoving the businessman. The situation was escalating. Others in the car had frightened looks on their faces, but none of them did anything to help the businessman or me. A few raced off the train at the next stop, and others moved forward into the next car.

The pushing and shoving and shouting continued. All the while, the businessman kept saying to me, "I won't leave you. I won't leave you." And the mugger kept saying, "Everything's cool, man. I'm sorry. I just need a couple of bucks."

The mugger kept reaching into his pockets, which made me question whether he had a knife or gun. I finally asked, "If I give you a couple of bucks, will you go away?" He growled back, "Make it a five or ten," and at that, I knew if I pulled my wallet from my shoe, he would take it and run with it— credit cards, driver's license, cash, everything would be taken.

I didn't know what to do. I thought, *If we could just get away from this guy*, but at the same time, I knew that if we got off at the next stop, the mugger could easily follow us and there might not be people around to help.

The train made two more stops, but no one came to our aid. Finally at the third stop, the mugger was so annoyed with the businessman, he tried to drag him off the train. He hit the businessman squarely across the nose, which caused a gush of blood. At that moment, a security guard on the platform saw the assault and rushed into the car. The mugger bolted, and another guard ran after him.

Both the businessman and I were shaken, to say the least, as we settled back into our seats. A woman came to the aid of the businessman with tissues for his bleeding nose. We eventually calmed down, gathered our wits about us, and began to converse. As it turned out, my helper was an attorney, and he was also on his way to the airport. I thanked him profusely for his help and assumed that we would part ways as soon as we got to the airport. He insisted, however, in walking with me all the way to my departure gate, even though his flight was scheduled to depart from another terminal and his nose was still bleeding.

I am forever grateful to this man. He may very well have spared me serious injury or worse. He took a major hit on my behalf. As I learned later, his nose was actually broken by the mugger's punch.

If you ever find yourself ceasing to feel grateful for the help others give you, take note. You may have become so accustomed to taking from others that you feel entitled to their help. People who feel that others owe them help are likely to be self-focused manipulators.

When someone offers you help, whether you accept it or not, thank the person for extending the offer. Be grateful that another person cares enough about you as a human being to assist you. Saying "thank you" is far more than a polite courtesy. It's an expression of affirmation to another person. When you give affirmation, you nearly always receive affirmation in return.

In the end, we all desperately need one another, not merely to have company on the planet, but to realize our potential and to have a sense of fulfillment and purpose in life.

Today might be the day for you to park yourself in front of your mirror and take another hard look at who you are and what you have been gifted to be and to do. Sure, you may see some flaws. There may be some age and some wear and tear. But look again. Look at the possibilities!

Fourteen

WHEN I WAS TWENTY-FOUR YEARS OLD, I PROUDLY unlocked the door and walked across the threshold of *my* home.

In the time I worked for the Zig Ziglar Corporation, I traveled so much that I never felt truly at home in my apartment. I had no desire to purchase a home, only to worry about its security and upkeep while I was on the road. After two and a half years of living in Dallas, I had become a little road weary, and I felt ready to return home to Breese and put down *roots*.

I already had deep roots in Breese. Most of the townspeople know who I am, know what I am capable of doing, and accept both my strengths and my limitations. The roots I had there were ones from my past. I felt ready to put down roots that would be part of my future.

I rented an apartment in Breese and almost immediately began to look for a home to buy. Throughout the winter, I spent most of my Saturdays and evenings searching the classified ads and driving through neighborhoods, old ones that were familiar to me and new ones that developed while I was away at college and at work in Dallas.

Breese is a small town, and there are only so many homes for sale at any given time. Some of the houses were ones that needed extensive work, which I wasn't eager to do or to pay someone else to do. Other houses just weren't my style or were unsatisfactory in one way or another. After four months of house hunting, I was exasperated.

Then one March morning, I expressed my frustration to Jeanie Steinman, co-owner of the local body shop where I was having my car repaired. When I went to pick up my car, we chatted casually, and I mentioned that I was disappointed that I hadn't been able to find just the right house to buy. I asked her if she had heard of any houses that were coming up for sale. She threw out some ideas, but I had already eliminated the houses she mentioned. Then she said in a rather sarcastic voice, "Well, you could buy that big old house on the north side that nobody wants!"

My mind went blank for a moment. What house was she talking about? Then I remembered a large washed-out yellow-and-white Victorian in the old section of town. A realtor had mentioned the property to me a couple of months earlier, but we had discounted the house immediately because of its age and size.

"No way," I responded. "I need that place like a hole in the head." We laughed and I drove away.

The next Sunday I was heading out to my parents' home on the road that led past the old Victorian. As I sped by, I recalled Jeanie's jest to buy it. I shook my head at the thought of such an idea. But suddenly a weird feeling came over me. I jerked my car into a hard left turn and drove around the block to take a closer look at the place. I parked my car across the street and peered for some time at the house. I didn't just look at the house. I took time to *see* the house.

The age was apparent. The paint on the clapboards was peeling in some areas. The ornamental trees and bushes were overgrown. Even so, the majesty of the old house was evident to me.

Four hefty Ionic columns supported the wraparound porch. A richly colored oval stained-glass window was located next to the front door. A handmade copper finial of flowers capped the steeple of the forty-foot turret.

I was especially drawn to the gigantic tree at the side of the house. Its brawny limbs reached out like huge arms that seemed to hug the house. Even though the tree had dense deep-purple leaves, I couldn't help noticing the massive trunk. The wrinkles and gnarls of the gray bark added character to the tree. It was obvious the tree's roots ran deep.

A few branches of the tree nearly touched the ground as other limbs sprawled high above the home's third story. The massive trunk and the fragile sprouts of new green life at the tips of the limbs stood in sharp contrast. I felt certain that the tree had witnessed countless family members and friends coming and going through the front door of the old house. It was a comforting thought.

Something about the longevity of the house and the tree conveyed permanence to me. Words like *solid*, *traditional*, *stately*, *neglected but worthy of restoring*, and *historic* came to mind. So did the word *roots*.

As I looked at the tree and studied every exterior detail of the house's facade, I heard Jeanie's voice in my mind. She had described it as "the house nobody wants." Indeed, it had been on the market for nearly a year. The more I looked at the property, the more I felt a little sorry for the old house.

Sorry for it, but nevertheless attracted to it. I recalled brief memories from my childhood when we had passed the house in our family car as Dad drove us to school. I had fantasized even as a young boy about what it would be like to live in such a big house. I think the structure probably reminded me of the Fisher-Price and Lego castles that I had spent hours building when I was a child.

I finally concluded, *It needs some work, but it could again stand in glory.*

At that point, I brought myself sharply back to reality. New thoughts replaced the images of restoration: *I'm only a single guy. That's way too much house for me. How would I maintain such an old house? It would need considerable maintenance. Owning such a home would be impractical and ridiculous. I can't swing a hammer or stand on a ladder to paint. Besides, I probably can't afford it.*

I drove on and turned my attention to the time ahead with my family.

Over the next several days, however, thoughts of the house kept popping into my mind. I visualized painting the house in a bold, classy color scheme. I envisioned how I would manicure the yard. As each of these fantasies began to develop, I'd tell myself to forget the idea. And each time I tried to forget the idea, I found myself driving back by the house.

I finally realized that the only way I was ever going to get the romantic notion of owning this home out of my head was to check out its interior condition and the owner's asking· price. I convinced myself, *When I find out how much work the place needs and how much it costs, I'll get over it.*

One foot into the entry of the house, and I was swept away. The large foyer pulled me inside, and the heavy wooden staircase invited me to climb it. As I walked from room to room, I discovered that the house was not at all in disrepair. To the contrary, it was in remarkably good condition. The previous owner had equipped the house with central air-conditioning, and it had been completely rewired. All of my excuses about interior restoration faded away. I truly felt "at home."

I talked to my banker, my attorney, and then my accountant. The only professional I didn't consult was my brother, the insurance agent. I was afraid to say anything to my family. I feared they would tell me I was nuts and talk me out of buying the house.

All through my childhood, whenever someone told me I couldn't do something, I became all the more determined to tackle the challenge. I didn't want this to be something I did just to prove a point. I was looking for the right house for *me*, and I knew it was a decision I needed to make for myself.

Armed with as much information as I could gather, I began to negotiate with the owner. We went back and forth with various offers, and at 4:30 on a Saturday afternoon, we agreed on a price.

I was ecstatic. The house was mine! I couldn't contain my excitement. I just had to tell somebody that I was a new home owner. Since my parents were out of town for the weekend, I ran down to my friend Neil's house, woke him up from a nap, and shared my victory with him. I'm not sure he was all that excited about being awakened, but he was a good sport in helping me celebrate this event that seemed like a milestone accomplishment to me.

As soon as my parents returned home, I broke the news to them.

Mom was speechless.

After a moment, she raised her right hand to brush a tear from her cheek and sputtered, "Of all my sons, I can't believe you bought that house. I can't believe you bought the very house I gave up . . . for you."

It was the first time I had heard the story about Mom and Dad wanting to buy *this very house* and then walking away from the deal because they couldn't envision how their son born with seven congenital disabilities would ever be able to manage climbing three flights of stairs.

I think about that story in my parents' life from time to time as I climb the thirty-two steps from the ground floor to the third-floor master bedroom suite. Steps they doubted I would ever be able to climb are part of my daily routine. The house they adored, but sacrificed for the sake of creating a home for me, is now the house I thoroughly enjoy calling my home.

After I moved into the house, Grandma sent me a letter.

Photo by Jim Kennett

John enjoying a quiet evening, reading at home in his restored house.

In it she wrote, "You are such a prize to me. I am proud of you, John . . . I didn't have much faith when you were born, but I must admit [my faith] surely has gotten stronger."

Are you looking for your own future today?

Are you discouraged that you don't see much opportunity or much potential or much that is positive?

Are you struggling with opinions that others have placed around you like a smothering blanket—opinions such as "You can't do it," "That's not for you," "You'll never be able to afford that," or "There'd be too much effort involved in preparing yourself for that career or the accomplishment of that goal."

I encourage you to park yourself in front of your life for a while and take another hard look at who you are and what you have been gifted to be and to do. Sure, there may be some flaws. There may be some age. There may be some wear and tear.

But take a look at the possibilities! How might things be changed? Fixed up? Restored? Renewed? Made better?

Allow yourself to dream again. Allow yourself to see a new future for yourself—one that will allow you to grow and expand and put down deep roots into the good soil of faith, love, and satisfying relationships with family members and friends.

Expand your vision.

Look for new options.

And then recognize that the choice to act is yours.

People are like stained-glass windows. They glow and sparkle when it's sunny and bright; but when the sun goes down their true beauty is revealed only if there is a light from within.

– Author unknown

Fifteen

HOW DO YOU CHOOSE TO WALK YOUR DAILY JOURNEY?

ONE DAY MY NEPHEW NICHOLAS'S FIRST-GRADE teacher showed Nick and his classmates my video, *Armed with Hope*. The children were mesmerized as they watched me crack eggs with my feet and sign autographs holding a fountain pen between my toes.

When Nicholas got home that afternoon, he asked his mother, "Why does Uncle John have a movie?"

Surprised by Nick's question, Denise searched for a simple answer. "I guess because Uncle John doesn't have any arms."

Nick shrugged his shoulders and then turned and walked away, muttering as he went, "What's so great about that?"

When Denise told me what Nicholas had said, we both had a good laugh. I was glad to learn that my condition is no big deal to Nick. I doubt that he even thinks it's odd that I use my toes as he uses his fingers. He has never known me to function in any other way. Throughout that day I chuckled every time I thought about what Nick had said. He was more right than he knew.

There actually is nothing great about not having arms. A

lack of arms is *not* the fact of my life that determines greatness, just as it is *not* the fact of my life that dictates automatic failures.

What I hope *is* great about my life is the way in which I have overcome and continue to overcome this condition in my life.

What I hope *is* great is my attitude toward my condition and the ways in which I have learned to look beyond my physical condition and tackle the real conditions of my inner life.

What I hope *is* great is my desire to fulfill my potential and my purpose in life, both of which are affected by my condition but neither limited nor defined by it.

When I speak to groups of children, they often ask, "How long did it take you to learn how to overcome your disability?"

The truth is, I haven't learned everything yet. I am continually learning how to overcome my condition. There's always something new to learn. There's always a new challenge on the horizon. Just when I think I have one difficulty licked, it seems to sneak up and taunt me from another angle.

Living is like climbing a range of mountains. Just when I get to the top of one mountain, I look to the horizon and see another even higher peak that dares me to conquer it.

No, I have not fully overcome my condition. Rather, I am in a constant state of overcoming it. I face a constant struggle. Nothing about my physical condition is in the past tense. I live daily without arms, and I live daily with challenges related to a lack of arms. I take life one step at a time. And I take those steps with an overcoming attitude.

You may not be able to totally overcome lots of things in your life. You may continually be faced with problems that are related to permanent physical features or that are the consequence of a failure in judgment or a failure of effort. There's no excuse, however, for choosing to live with a defeatist, negative attitude.

Are there still moments when I feel left out? Certainly. I'd love to be able to join my friends and participate fully in their Sunday afternoon golf outings. I'd like to be able to help my brothers and their buddies hang drywall as part of a home-remodeling team of helpers.

Are there still moments when I feel rejected? Of course. Like most guys, I don't like being turned down when I ask a girl for a date.

Are there still moments when I am fearful? Sure. I don't like to think about the possibility of getting arthritis in my hip joints, which would severely limit my ability to use my legs.

Are there still moments when I feel awkward? Every time I try something new that requires physical or emotional risk taking!

I simply choose not to dwell on the things about which I can do nothing. I enjoy the times I *do* share with friends and family members. I take pleasure in the times when I can assist my brothers. I do what I can to keep my joints limber and healthy. I still take the risk of asking out attractive women. I still swallow my pride and take risks even when I feel awkward.

I know I'm not alone in not arriving. I've talked to countless people who have admitted, "I thought I had learned how to be patient, but then a situation came up and here I am again, struggling with my impatience." Or "I thought I had learned how to say no to too many projects, but here I am again, swamped by work." Or "I thought I had my schedule balanced, but here I am again, overextended in just the area in which I was trying to cut back the hours."

Every stage of life offers new challenges. The very process of aging offers new challenges. Every new level of maturity, commitment, fame, or accomplishment offers new challenges. There's no arriving, and at the same time, there's no quitting.

MY DAILY PRAYER FOR THE JOURNEY

Every day, I seek to walk out the journey of my life with four things:

1. A vision of hope

2. A calmness rooted in patience

3. A gritty determination to persevere

4. An intimate relationship with God through prayer

These are the foundation stones on which I establish my commitment to living out a life marked by excellence and meaningful purpose.

1. A Vision of Hope

Hope is not a destination. It is the atmosphere in which I walk toward a destination. Hope gives me a reason to get out of bed in the morning and to make the journey. Hope is the expectancy that it *is* possible for me to live a day, a month, a year, an entire lifetime that is satisfying, fulfilling, joyful, and meaningful.

Hope is not pie-in-the-sky wishful thinking or fantasy. It is rooted in truth viewed through the lens of objectivity. Objectivity results in options, and options give rise to hope. Real hope is never vague. Ambiguity results in discouragement, not hope. Real hope is based upon what genuinely might be. It is based upon what can be defined, seen, and envisioned. The more specific the outcome anticipated, the stronger the feelings of hope for achieving it.

2. Calm Patience

Not everything can be done in a day. Not everything can even be planned or envisioned in a day. We are called to walk out a journey called life, putting one foot in front of the other and walking with steadiness and faithfulness.

I encounter many people who are both hurried and harried. They are enthusiastic, even frantic, about arriving at the success of their lives. As they bustle from one activity to the next, one event to the next, one project to the next, they seem to lose sight of the fact that we cannot make all things happen. Some things happen to us, both good and bad, that are beyond our control. We need to be able to walk through the bad times with perseverance and endurance. We need to be able to slow down enough to truly enjoy the good times and to share them with family and friends.

We cannot control most circumstances or situations, but we can control our responses to them. I choose to be a patient observer of many things—curious to see how they will unfold in God's providential plan. I do what I know to do and what I can do. I leave the rest in the hands of others and ultimately in the hands of God.

3. Gritty Determination

I have a scar on my chin that I acquired as a toddler learning to walk. Without arms to brace myself or cushion a fall, my chin regularly seemed to hit the floor, driveway, and bathtub as I learned to walk, run, climb stairs, and maneuver my body into various positions. If my parents had been afraid to let me fall, they would never have given me the encouragement to walk. I take that same approach toward my life now.

I am determined to succeed in my goals, the foremost of which is to live a life that is deeply meaningful, a life of service to others, a life that gives me a feeling of personal satisfaction. I am determined to persevere in accomplishing what I set out to accomplish. I know that I will have times when I fall, falter, or fail. That's life. I refuse to stay down, however, when those times occur. I choose to get up, regain my balance, and move forward.

4. Intimacy with God Through Prayer

I know that I do not walk life's path alone. I do not believe that God necessarily rolls out the red carpet or opens doors in advance of our births. I am convinced that He walks down our path in life with us. He guarantees us that He is beside us all the way. What more can a person ask?

Whenever I find myself feeling fearful or doubtful about my future, I take comfort in the words of the apostle Paul: "All things work together for good to those who love God, to those who are the called according to His purpose" (Rom. 8:28). Paul did not say that everything that happens is good; rather, God picks up the broken pieces of life and creates something good. Just as the broken fragments of glass make up the beautiful stained-glass window by my front door, God takes the broken shards of our lives and puts them together in something that brings Him pleasure and allows His light to radiate through us to others.

As long as I can remember, this statement has hung in my mother's stairwell: "People are like stained-glass windows. They glow and sparkle when it's sunny and bright; but when the sun goes down their true beauty is revealed only if there is a light from within."

More than anything, I want the light of God to shine in me so that others might take courage from my example and grow in their faith.

Conclusion

THE ANSWERS ARE YOURS

MANY OF US HAVE PLAYED THE GAME TWENTY Questions. In this book, I have asked you fifteen probing questions that I believe are worthy of answers—not just any answers, not the answers of a professional adviser, but *your* answers.

1. Are your actions speaking louder than your feelings?
2. How are you dealing with your condition?
3. Are you willing to do the last thing you want to do?
4. Do you genuinely love yourself enough to change yourself?
5. What's your style?
6. What position are you playing in the game of life?
7. How do you feel about your chances at making the play-offs?
8. How big a life are you willing to pursue?
9. Have you laughed at yourself lately?
10. Are you asking the right questions?
11. Are you spiraling downward or upward?

12. Are you aware that you are blessed to be a blessing?

13. Are you willing to ask for help?

14. Is there a new possibility you need to explore?

15. How do you choose to walk your daily journey?

Your answers will determine not only your future, but also the degree of joy, fulfillment, and satisfaction you enjoy in your life. Your answers will affect you and everyone who loves you.

All problems have solutions, but you must do the seeking.

All things are within reach, but you must do the reaching.

ACKNOWLEDGMENTS

I wish to recognize those individuals who helped make my dream of writing this book a reality:

Vicky Albers—my friend and fellow writer. Your interest in my story inspired me to start writing. Also, meeting with me once a month to brainstorm and review my progress kept me on course.

Pam Bores—my friend and archivist. Your tireless efforts to catalog and preserve all of my newspaper articles and memorabilia helped me to easily rediscover facts, stories, events, and quotations about my life that enriched this book. In addition, lending me your caring ear allowed me to articulate and transform verbal ideas into the printed word.

Carol Dolan and Dan Williams—my friends and test readers. By reading and rereading the manuscript, each of you gave me valuable feedback about the tone, clarity, and usefulness of this book.

Patrick and Paul Foppe—my brothers and toughest critics. You both held me to the highest standard of writing. Through your candor, you guys challenged me to dig deeper and think harder to find the most insightful experiences and information that would give others real hope.

Tina Klostermann—my executive assistant. You patiently "lent me a hand" with so many logistical issues of this book including typing, copying, researching, and proofreading.

Jay Memmott, Ph.D.—my professor. You taught me to examine psychological and relationship issues from various perspectives, and you made certain that my material was clinically valid.

Zig Ziglar—my mentor. You recognized my potential talents as a speaker and graciously gave me a platform to share my message with the world. I thank God for bringing us together, and I am forever grateful for all the opportunities you have opened for me. I pray that I will always live up to your expectations to remain a humble and effective motivator.

ABOUT THE AUTHOR

PROFESSIONAL SPEAKER JOHN FOPPE WAS BORN without arms. He delivers high-impact presentations on handling life's oldest struggles, such as feeling good about yourself, staying motivated, dealing with negative people, and doing more with less. He uses his heartwarming and humorous stories of overcoming adversity to educate and motivate others.

He holds a master's degree in social work from St. Louis University. In addition, John is a protégé of motivational speaker and author Zig Ziglar. In 1993, the U.S. Junior Chamber of Commerce recognized John as one of the "Ten Outstanding Young Americans." This prestigious award recognizes young leaders for their positive contributions to society.

John is a committed Christian. His public speaking mission started fifteen years ago after he experienced a spiritual awakening during a missionary trip to Haiti. John remains active in his Catholic parish. He has been a volunteer youth minister and has served in various lay leadership roles.

Today, John operates his own international seminar business and travels throughout the world speaking to all types of businesses, churches, and organizations.

To contact John about delivering a seminar for your group:

John Foppe Seminars, Inc.
P.O. Box 94
Breese, IL 62230

or

www.johnfoppe.com

On May 13, 1995, God called Zig Ziglar's oldest daughter, Suzan, home. Journeying through his own grief, Ziglar realized many things about himself, his family, his priorities, and God. In this comforting book, he uses his experience to encourage you to deal with the reality of loss and learn to take up the threads of life again as you find consolation and inspiration in the Giver of All Peace.

ISBN 0-7852-6855-3

In this repackaged bestseller John Maxwell examines the differences between leadership styles, outlines principles for inspiring, motivating, and influencing others. These principles can be used in any organization to foster integrity and self-discipline and bring a positive change.

Developing the Leader Within You also allows readers to examine how to be effective in the highest calling of leadership by understanding the five characteristics that set "leader managers" apart from "run-of-the-mill managers."

In this John Maxwell classic, he shows readers how to develop the vision, value, influence, and motivation required of successful leaders.

ISBN 0-7852-6666-6

It has been said that when the going gets tough, the hopeful keep going. That's because hope is the great activator—in other words, people with it take action to realize their goals. But many times the daily grind can be a hope-killer, so Zig Ziglar offers a solution! Ziglar encourages us to spend five minutes every morning with *Staying Up, Up, Up in a Down, Down World*, thus gaining the inspiration and encouragement needed to face daily obstacles.

Full of hope-inspiring vignettes from Ziglar, words of encouragement from well-known leaders, and Scripture for meditation and prayer, this quick read provides the motivation needed for meeting your goals and fulfilling your dreams.

ISBN 0-7852-7077-9

ARMED WITH HOPE

Closed Captioned
Format: VHS
Length: 30 minutes

Price: $49.95

JOHN FOPPE WAS BORN WITHOUT ARMS. HIS disability has given him a unique perspective on life. *Armed with Hope* takes you behind the scenes into the everyday life of this remarkable man as he shares his hopes, fears, and dreams.

Discover how an armless man handles tasks that most of us take for granted, like driving a car or cracking an egg. You'll meet John's parents, who share how "tough love" played an important role in shaping John's values and attitude toward life.

John's story is an inspirational example of how to turn stumbling blocks into stepping-stones for a brighter future.

John P. Foppe
SEMINARS, INC.
®

To order: Visit www.johnfoppe.com